Looking Into The Pain

D.L Johnson

Copyright © 2024 by D.L Johnson

All rights reserved. No part of this publication may be reproduced, distributed, or transmitted in any form or by any means, including photocopying, recording, or other electronic or mechanical methods, without the prior written permission of the publisher, except in the case of brief quotations embodied in critical reviews and certain other noncommercial uses permitted by copyright law.

Table of Contents

Dedicated to Little Gracie
Your life and love changed me forever.

A gratitude of thanks
To my husband Warren, who has sacrificed a lot of time for me to seek my dreams.
To Ms. Yvette, you have shown me love, support, encouragement, and always believed in me.
To LiQuiche for guiding me through this entire process, and sharing your tools, and feedback.
To Chardythe for the lovely artwork. You truly have a gift.

Introduction

Looking into the pain is a difficult and daunting experience. However, healing comes during and through this process. No one I know likes pain whether it is physical, mental, or emotional. Most people try to avoid pain at all costs. To do this we try to self-soothe using sleeping pills, illicit drugs, alcohol, food, shopping, keeping busy, and other things that will help us avoid the discomfort. Although we see pain as something to avoid, it is actually a good thing. When we have pain in the body, it is the body's way of letting us know something is not quite right and to pay attention. When we have emotional pain, our spirit is letting us know that we have some areas of our heart and soul that need to be acknowledged and healed. It is through pain that God grabs our attention which sends us to our knees. Pain gives us the capacity we need to understand that we cannot do life without Him. It does this by removing all distractions that keep us from this fact. Pain draws our attention to the source of the pain. When we stub our toe, the whole body responds, and our only focus is bringing comfort to the toe. That's physical pain, but the same happens with emotional pain. If our heart is broken, it can literally feel like the beating heart in our chest is hurting. We can't think or focus on anything else but the anguish we feel. Because of the immensity of our pain, we turn to God.

I learned that without pain there is no growth. When we grow, it means we are being elevated or moved from one place to another. This can be physically, mentally, or spiritually. Because we don't like change, it feels like pain. We like that which we are familiar with. We don't like the uneasy and vulnerable feelings change requires. This uneasy, awkward, vulnerable place is the catalyst for this book.

2023

The Holy Spirit began the work of tilling the hardened garden of my heart. He picked and pulled away some thick, impacted dirt that had been embedded for years. The process was tedious and arduous. It was painful, scary, and heart-wrenching. The process included some devastating experiences. Things that would change how I saw myself, how I saw God, my perspective on life and my purpose, and relationships I held dear. It would change even my professional life. I went through a breaking process. What is "a breaking"? It is when God strips us of our pride and self-sufficiency that the character of Jesus can shine through. The breaking allows true healing to take place. If a broken finger is not cared for properly, it may reset incorrectly causing it to heal but appear crooked or deformed. In order for the deformity to be corrected, an orthopedic surgeon must rebreak the finger and align the bones so that it repairs correctly. This is what was happening to me throughout 2023. I was being broken so that God could reset me. It was one of the hardest undertakings I have had to endure. Going through this process showed me how life is fleeting. "... For you are a mist that appears for a little time and vanishes." James 4:14. I learned that I needed God then and now in a much bigger way than I realized. Life changes, but God does not. Life and everything on earth are temporary, but God is not; He is eternal. He is in complete control. He cannot change. He cannot be manipulated. He loves me so much that He is willing to break me to change me. My tears and my pleas cannot sway Him to change His love for me and the work that needs to take place on the inside of me. Because of the breaking, I am becoming new. He is molding me, building me into a beautiful new masterpiece.

As you experience pain, loss, change, or adversity, look for God. He is dependable and He loves you. Know that He is working in you to bring you to a place of completion in Him. He is crafting a masterpiece that is blameless and righteous. Don't let go of your faith. Don't let go of Him. "Don't be afraid for I am with you. Don't be discouraged, for I am your God. I will strengthen you. I will help you. I will hold onto you with my righteous right hand." Isaiah 41:10. And that is just what He showed me throughout that year of change. I was afraid, discouraged, and helpless. But, through it all, He showed up for me and he held me up when I could not and would not help myself. He orchestrated the breaking and the healing. While I am still going through it, I can look back over the year and see His hand in every part of the process. As a result, I feel blessed and highly favored. An amazing loving Father, who just so happens to be the Creator of the Universe, took time to break down this clay pot and begin the process of rebuilding it from the bottom up. When He is done, I will be a beautiful work of art. Now I understand when I used to hear the seasoned women say they were on the potter's wheel. It's my turn and, even though I am a little apprehensive, I know I am in the best hands.

Remember pain is an indication that something is happening in you to create change. Sit in the pain. Let it roll over you. Take the opportunity to allow God to sit with you to love and comfort you as He molds you into His beautiful artwork.

CHAPTER 1

Not My Emotions, My Knees

*On one occasion, Hannah got up after they ate and
drank at Shiloh ... 1 Sam 1:9*

Hannah is introduced to us in the first book of Samuel. She is married to Elkanah who was a descendant of the priestly tribe of Levi. Elkanah had two wives, Hannah whom he loved, and Peninnah. Hannah could not have children which greatly grieved her. Peninnah had many children and constantly held this fact over Hannah's head and used it to torment her to tears.

In this story, we get a front seat to Hannah's grief. We learn the reason she is unable to bear children. Is it something she did, or something that has been done to her? We see the series of emotions Hannah expresses and verbalizes and how she eventually manages this very difficult position she finds herself in. We observe how the dilemma not only affects her but also those around her. Finally, we glimpse the resolution of this very challenging season in her life. We get to witness her breaking process and the point of her surrender.

When God Allows Prolonged Anguish

Throughout this story, a picture is painted illuminating Hannah's vast emotions that she experiences as she looks at the cards that she has been dealt. Hannah was deeply distressed, and she wept bitterly 1 Sam 1:10; she was troubled in spirit (brokenhearted), 1 Sam 1:15; she expressed great anxiety (anguish), and vexation (resentment or grief), 1 Sam 1:16. She was in a tremendous amount of pain because of her unfulfilled desire to have children. And though she was experiencing this deep yearning and hurt inside, she also knew others were thinking she had brought this upon herself. In the first century, it was believed that women who were unable to get pregnant had unconfessed sin in their lives. It was considered a curse to be unable to bear children since that was a woman's primary role. This was important because these babies would grow up and have an obligation to care for their parents in their old age. Childless parents were pitied because their fate was bleak. There were no skilled nursing facilities or caregivers that would come to the homes of the elderly to make sure their needs were met.

It is amazing and hard to grasp the immensity of emotions we were masterfully created to express. Some emotions are wonderful and some, of course, are difficult, but we need them all. What does it say about God that He has given us such an array of emotions? One thing is for sure, He knows us and the emotions we feel. Why is this important? It is important because instead of coming to God with these safe prayers pretending and holding back our true emotions, we can be authentic and transparent, truthful. It is in the times when I have openly expressed myself to God that I have been closest to Him. It is in our nakedness before God that we find freedom. Our shame is extinguished when we bare our souls to Him.

During a period of grieving, I had lost faith in God's love for me. I felt that He could have protected me but didn't. I told Him that I believe He is sovereign and all-powerful and there was nothing that He could not do. My problem was that there are times when He would not protect me and had not protected me based on His will. I was so disappointed. I felt betrayed because I trusted God to protect me and those connected to me. I was deeply distressed, troubled in spirit, and bitter towards God. He knows the end from the beginning, so He already knew what was coming and He didn't stop it. I rumbled with God and my faith in Him. I asked Him, "How can I trust You to protect me when I know that if it's not Your will, You won't?" Talking about raw emotions, I knew He could see through me, and I thought, I might as well be honest with Him about how I was feeling. When you are hurting, and at the end of your rope, being nice and reserved will keep you bound to the place to which you are trying to get free.

Hannah's barrenness was assumed to be her fault. She as well as others thought she was not able to get pregnant because God was punishing her. This however was not the case. Hannah's barrenness was allowed so the work of God would be displayed in her life. "But to Hannah, he gave a double portion because he loved her, *though the Lord had closed her womb*, 1 Sam 1:5 (emphasis mine). "The Lord had closed her womb" is an interesting statement. We know only God can give life, so it is undeniable that God did not allow life to be conceived in Hannah. The statement is repeated in the next verse. "And her rival used to provoke her grievously to irritate her *because the Lord had closed her womb*", 1 Sam 1:6 (emphasis mine). Scripture emphasizes that Hannah's deficiency was done on purpose for a purpose. God would receive glory from Hannah's predicament. God will use our very hindrances, deficiencies, and pain to bring about His glory. In John 9:2-3, the disciples questioned Jesus about a man who had been blind since birth. They asked, "... who sinned, this man or his parents?" Isn't it amazing how we always look for who is at fault? Jesus told them, "Neither this man nor his parents sinned... but this happened so that the work of God might be displayed in his life." So it is with Hannah, that she was barren not because of wrongdoing but because God wanted to get glory from her life.

God Provides a Way to Endure

Hannah's inability to produce was not a curse. God blessed Hannah by giving her in marriage to Elkanah. "*... because he loved her*, though the Lord had closed her womb", 1 Sam 1:5 (emphasis mine). Elkanah loved Hannah so much that he was willing to suffer the ridicule he must have faced from the community because his wife could not bear him any children. He had every legal right to divorce Hannah but would not. Why would God attach Hannah to a man who loved her so much that he would risk his reputation and livelihood on a woman who could not provide him with children if He (God) was punishing her? To make up for her deficiency, Elkanah married Peninnah (not God's plan) to continue his family line. He did not marry Peninnah because he loved her but because he loved Hannah. Peninnah's only purpose in his life was to give him children. Hannah had Elkanah's heart and Peninnah had Elkanah's children. Both women wanted what the other had. How many of us have looked at someone else's life or situation and thought, "I wish I could have or do that?" We must be content with what God has blessed us with. He has given us what He knows we can handle. We may not be willing or able to endure what the person endured to get what they have.

The Struggle is Real

Peninnah was probably Hannah's slave. Often in the first century, when a wife was unable to bear children, the wife's slave would be given to the husband in marriage to continue the family line. One occasion of this was with Abram and Sarai who doubted when they were waiting on the promise of God to give them children. Sarai gave Hagar to Abram saying, "*...Go in to my servant*; it may be that I shall obtain children by her...," Genesis 16:2 (emphasis mine). This decision made by Abram and Sarai turned out horribly distressing for Sarai. Just like Peninnah, Hagar began to treat Sarai cruelly because she was able to bear children and her mistress was not. "... And when she (Hagar) saw that she had conceived, *she looked with contempt on her mistress*," Genesis 16:4 (emphasis mine). Peninnah is described as Hannah's rival. I am a person who loves words, so I like to use synonyms to help me understand exactly what a particular word means. I looked up the definition of rival to make sure I had a clear picture of the word. Rival means, competing with another for the same objective; an antagonist. I thought that was very interesting. What was Peninnah competing for? Did she believe that because she had Elkanah's children, he would fall in love with her instead of her mistress? Peninnah was so blindly jealous that she used her mistress' deepest pain to provoke her. To provoke means to deliberately incite an emotion; to taunt, irritate, or torment. Did Peninnah want to make Hannah cry or was she trying to get her to do something so horrible that Elkanah would replace Hannah with herself? Can you see Hannah's dilemma? The very slave that she gave to her husband to make her family better tormented her every year. "So it went on *year by year*. As often as she went up to the house of the Lord, she used to provoke her," 1 Sam 1:7 (emphasis mine). Just like Sarai and Abram, Hannah and Elkanah found themselves in a very distressing situation.

Shame Elevated

Elkanah loved Hannah despite her inability to give him children. Peninnah taunted her because of her inability to have children. Two different people in her life, one who loved her and one who despised her, were tearing Hannah apart. Elkanah wanted her to get over it. He wanted her to acknowledge the ways in which he was expressing his love for her. ".... Am I not more to you than ten sons?", 1 Sam 1:8. Peninnah wanted to shame and humiliate her. Hannah had her own internal suffering and these two, Elkanah and Peninnah, added to her anguish. Elkanah, however, was motivated by his love for her. He wanted her to be happy and well. He needed her to understand that he did not marry her for children but because he loved her. Even still, the pressure of your spouse expecting you to let go of the very dream you've had since you were a little girl, is heart-wrenching. It is what women are supposed to do. She felt inadequate, insufficient, incomplete, and defective. She did not need Peninnah to torment her, she was already doing that to herself. That is why it was so easy for Peninnah to upset her. We can know something about ourselves, like being overweight, but when someone else mentions it, it is like a kick in the gut. I used to eat my food really fast. This was a result of being one of eight children and living a poor life where food was scarce. When we sat down for meals, I had to eat quickly because if I turned my head or left the table, my food would be gobbled up by one of my siblings and I would just be hungry until the next meal. Well, one day I hung out with my then-boyfriend's family at their fish fry. I did what I would normally do. I fixed my plate and within five minutes, my food was gone. My boyfriend's sister said, "Wow, do you want more food?" I was so embarrassed that I could not enjoy the rest of the family gathering. I knew I would gobble up my food before everyone else but when someone mentioned it, just like Hannah, my shame was elevated. I am still self-conscious when eating with other people.

Lord of Hosts

Hannah, still sad after forcing down the sacrificial meal with no joy, gets up and goes into the Temple to pray. "After they had eaten and drunk in Shiloh, *Hannah rose*," 1 Sam 1:9 (emphasis mine). Hannah GOT UP. She decided enough was enough, I'm not staying in this pain any longer. She was tired of her condition, so she went to the temple. Hannah's pain drove her to her knees. Hannah never acted out, her behavior was not boisterous or unbecoming. Yes, she cried and acted depressed, but she never took her discomfort out on other people. Instead, she prayed. This shows her faith in God although He had allowed a predicament in her life that brought her great agony. She still believed that God was righteous, merciful, and powerful. She cried out to the Lord of Hosts. Another term for the Lord of Hosts is the Lord of Armies. She did not call on God as the healer or provider, instead, she appealed to the attribute of God as a mighty army, the One who has never lost a battle. An army fights battles and defends those it is protecting. She wanted God to show His power by giving her a son.

I remember when me and my husband found large lumps on the body of our dog, Lady. We took her to our veterinarian. The look on his face told us it wasn't good. He gave us a prognosis of six to nine months for her to live. Me and my husband did not accept her fate based on the diagnosis from the veterinarian because we knew the Lord of Armies. I cried out to God with all the bravery I had in my body. I asked God to show Himself strong. I said, "I want to see your Power." In essence, I was saying the same thing Hannah said. We were calling God out and saying, "Show us what you got." While we did eventually lose Lady, it was almost four years later. I believe this is why I was sad but not devastated. God had shown up and showed out for me and I was grateful. Hannah not only wanted God to see her pain and respond, but she also wanted protection from her tormentor. She knew that once she was able to conceive and birth a child, it would shut the mouth of her rival.

Remember Me and Don't Forget Me

Hannah cried out to God in deep despair. She was at the end of herself, and she knew no one could help her but God. "And she vowed a vow and said, O Lord of hosts, if you will indeed look on the affliction of your servant and *remember me and not forget your servant*, but will give to your servant a son, then I will give him to the Lord all the days of his life, and no razor shall touch his head," 1 Sam 1:11 (emphasis mine). There is a lot in this one verse. First, she calls on God's attribute as an army to fight for her. Then she says something that to the naked eye, may not make sense. She says, "... look on the affliction of your servant and remember me and not forget your servant..." Is God not One who can see all things, is he senile and forgets? No. She was telling the Lord to stop neglecting her and answer her prayers. Pay attention to her pain and fulfill her request. What she did not realize, and we often don't realize, is that God's plan is perfect. Hannah had to suffer. God had to delay her request because the plan He had was not ready to be fulfilled yet. God had to wait until she was ready to give up the very thing she was asking for. She was so desperate, that she was willing to give the son she was asking God for back to Him. If He had fulfilled her request any sooner, Samuel would not have been promised to God as a Nazarite (consecrated for God's use). Samuel went on to be a great priest and judge for God's people.

The thing that you desire so much that it hurts, may be a desire that God has given you. But he is waiting on you to completely surrender yourself and that very desire to Him. We must remember everything we have has been given to us. Our intellect, our bodies, our spiritual gifts and talents, our homes, family, friends, and children have all been given to us by a merciful God. Are you willing to give back to Him all that He has given to you as an act of gratefulness and worship? We do not belong to ourselves and nothing we have is ours, we are only stewards and Hannah understood that. His plans are perfect, and we must trust Him. "For this light *momentary affliction* is preparing for us an eternal weight of glory beyond all comparison," 2 Corinthians 4:17 (emphasis mine). Hannah's momentary affliction was small compared to what God had in store for her. I can imagine the pride she must have had looking at her son who ruled a nation. I'm sure that although she remembers her pain and what she went through, in the end, it was all worth it. God is so amazing!

My heart exults in the Lord; my horn is exalted in the Lord. My mouth derides my enemies because I rejoice in your salvation. There is none holy like the LORD: for there is none besides you; there is no rock like our God. Talk no more so very proudly, let not arrogance come from your mouth; for the LORD is a God of knowledge, and by him actions are weighed. The bows of the mighty are broken, but the feeble bind on strength. Those who were full have hired themselves out for bread, but those who were hungry have ceased to hunger. The barren has borne seven. But she who has many children is forlorn. The LORD kills and brings to life; he brings down to Sheol and raises up. The LORD makes poor and makes rich; he brings low and he exalts. He raises up the poor from the dust; he lifts the needy from the ash heap to make them sit with princes and inherit a seat of honor. For the pillars of the earth are the LORD's, and on them he has set the world. He will guard the feet of his faithful ones, but the wicked shall be cut off in darkness, for not by might shall a man prevail. The adversaries of the LORD shall be broken into pieces; against them he will thunder in heaven. The LORD will judge the ends of the earth; he will give strength to his king and exalt the horn of his anointed.

1 Samuel 2:1-11

Reflection Questions

1. Compare a time when you have been authentic and forthright with God and a time when you came to Him with surface prayers. What was the result and at which time did you sense a closeness to God?

2. Do you have someone that tries to provoke you? When it occurs, what is your immediate response? Do you tend to lash out, cower, or try to have compassion?

3. Do you have a shame-spot? An area where you know you struggle but can deal with until someone brings it to your attention. It can be a weight problem, anger issues, addiction, etc.)

4. Describe a time when you reached a breaking point and all you knew to do was cry out to God for help.

5. Have you ever felt like God had forgotten about you? When? How did this feeling
    affect you? What did you do?

____

____

____

____

CHAPTER 2

Not Too Proud to Beg

"Yes, Lord," she said, "yet even the dogs eat the
crumbs that fall from their master's table."
Matthew 15:27

Jesus and the disciples were traveling from Gennesaret to Gentile territory, Tyre, and Sidon. They were looking for a place to lay low and rest. When they got to that region, a Canaanite woman, Mark's Gospel calls her a Syrophoenician woman, approached them. In fact, Jesus and the disciples had barely stepped foot in that region when she accosted them. The Christian Standard Bible (CSB) version states, "And behold" meaning "Check this out". It is as if she had been waiting for Jesus. She may have recognized them from afar as they were walking through town. They were Jews, so they would have stood out in a crowd of people, because of their attire. She must have heard about Jesus' compassion to heal others because she began to desperately cry out repeatedly "Jesus, Son of David, have mercy on me; my daughter is severely oppressed by a demon." I find it absolutely incredible, and I'm sure Jesus did too, how in His own region and among His own people He was continually asked to prove Himself as the Son of God. He was goaded and tested by the chief priests as well as others to make them believe He was the Messiah who came to save the world. This is a complete contrast to the Canaanite woman, a gentile, who had no rights to Jesus. Not only did she believe who He was, she pleaded with Him to help her. While Jesus' own people were turning their noses up at

Him, the Canaanite woman was honoring, worshipping, and leaning on the God-Man, the Savior, the one who would have compassion on her.

I can relate to Jesus in that the people closest to you don't acknowledge and understand who you are. I remember coming to the realization that the Holy Spirit had given me the gift to operate in the Office of a Prophet. I did not ask for this gift but nonetheless, it is what He gave me. I didn't even know what a prophet was, much less understand what I was supposed to do with the gift. As I studied and sought God for revelation, He began to show me that I had been operating in this very gift for some time and just didn't know it. The people closest to me could not see me and some refused to see me. There were jokes made about me behind my back and to my face. Unlike Jesus who boldly walked in who He was, I cowered. I wanted to hide so I would not continually be questioned and ridiculed about something I did not ask for or quite understand. Jesus knew exactly who He was and what His purpose was. He never let others diminish or detract from what He had come to do.

Persistent But Disregarded

The Canaanite woman, I'll call her Rebecca, was persistent in her cries for mercy. However, Jesus would not answer her pleas. I can see her shouting at the group of them, and Jesus never looking her way or acknowledging her. As I ponder this scene, I think about how I would feel if I was calling out to Jesus and He ignored me. I would be offended that the man everyone had been raving about, the man who supposedly had compassion on others to heal, restore, and renew, had disregarded me. Oh wait, I do that now. Let's be real, you do too. When we are in pain or need and we pray, if God does not answer us in what we feel is a timely manner, we get fed up and try to fix it ourselves. Or, better yet, when we try to do it ourselves instead of going to Him first, we make a mess. Then, we go to Him to fix it. If He does not pick up our pieces when we want Him to, we get annoyed, offended, upset, angry, and think He is ignoring us. This was not the case for Rebecca. She was more concerned about getting help for her daughter than her bruised ego. So, she persisted.

The disciples began to get annoyed at her incessant cries. I guess they had hoped that she would eventually give up and go away. Essentially, she had no rights to Jesus anyway. Rebecca was not concerned that she did not belong to the family of Abraham, Isaac, and Jacob. She had a need that she refused to let go unfulfilled. Has there been a time when you needed something so badly, that you refused to take no for an answer, or you refused to accept the answer you received? The disciples were indignant and aggravated at this woman's insolence to pester them. It is mind-blowing that not one of the disciples had compassion for her.

This event would be a lesson not only for Rebecca but also for the disciples. They had not learned the lesson of compassion and acceptance, even after Jesus had shown them examples. One example is the Woman at the well. She was a Samaritan, a half-breed for which the Jews hated. Jesus showed her great compassion regardless of her ethnicity and her circumstances. During my teenage years there was an epidemic of teen pregnancy and I happened to be one of the cases. I got pregnant at 14 years old, and I got to see how my church family really felt. I was no longer the loved young intellect but was looked down upon. I remember the faces. They were not caring and compassionate faces, but ones of disdain and rebuke. I learned in that season that some church people can be condemning and unforgiving. This Samaritan woman was treated the same way by people in her culture. They looked upon her with contempt because she had been married and divorced several times and she was currently living with a man who was not her husband. I was hard enough on myself, and I didn't need the criticism or the disapproving stares. We all find ourselves in a place where we need mercy and grace but when it is our turn to provide it to someone else, can we give the very thing we want to receive?

Sadly, with no empathy towards Rebecca who was fraught with fear for her daughter, the disciples asked Jesus to please do something. "... Send her away, for she is crying out after us." Matthew 15:23. It wasn't that she was crying out to them, she wanted Jesus. They were indifferent to her distress and concern for her daughter. They probably didn't care whether Jesus helped or not. They just wanted her to shut up and leave them alone.

Jesus continued without responding to Rebecca, but stated to the disciples, "… I was sent only to the lost sheep of the house of Israel." Matthew 15:24. The disciples may have thought, we know that Jesus, can you tell *her* so she can go away? It is baffling how we want others to have compassion for us and our loved ones, but we refuse to have compassion for others.

Giving It All You Got

Rebecca, having followed Jesus and His party into the house where they were seeking refuge, overheard their conversation. However, she had yet to be acknowledged. She had come to the realization that her cries for mercy had been discounted. In a last-ditch effort to get the attention of Jesus, she gave it all she had and fell on her knees at His feet. "But she came and knelt before him, saying, "Lord, help me." Matthew 15:25. On November 2022, I found a stray Bully-breed puppy while walking on a path near my home with my other two dogs, Sister, and Lulu. It was extremely cold, and the dog was on a dangerous street. I was so afraid that it could be hit by a car and killed. I left my two dogs where they were and climbed a fence to approach the dog. I approached cautiously because I didn't know if it was hurt, friendly, or just scared and I did not want to get bit or attacked. It was a girl dog, and she was shaking but allowed me to get close enough to pick her up. I put her on the other side of the fence where my two dogs were watching and waiting and then climbed back over the fence. She didn't have a collar on, so she was either lost or discarded. I was a long way from home, so I half carried her, and half walked her home with us. I fed her, bathed her, and after a month of trying to figure out who she belonged to, she became our new pet. We named her Gracie. She fit right into our family and me and my husband quickly fell in love with her. In January 2023, still being a puppy and not yet well trained, but very protective, she saw another dog across the street and charged over to investigate. She was killed by a passing car and my world came crashing down.

Today as I write this, it has been a little over six months and I am still trying to pick up the pieces as I grieve my miracle dog. I said all that to say, I understand when you get so desperate for help and you have reached your breaking point, sometimes all you can do is say, "Lord, help me." I said that over and over again as I grieved Gracie. It wasn't that I had not lost a dog before. In fact, five months before I found Gracie, we brought home the ashes of our very first dog, Lady. With Gracie, it was the tragic way in which she died, and I could not stop seeing her and thinking, she was just a baby and had no idea what was happening as the life began leaving her body. I loved that little baby so much that I cannot even express it in words. Rebecca was at a place past desperation just as I was in my grief. I am sure she would have given up her very life for her daughter, so to get on her knees and beg for Jesus' help was all she could think to do. It is in this place of raw emotion and surrender that God uses to change us. It is at this moment that chains break, addictions are overcome, and minds become renewed. It is a new beginning because getting to this place means there is only one way out, and that is up.

It was Rebecca on her knees in complete surrender that caused Jesus to move. She would no longer go on as unnoticed, overlooked, or ignored because she was in a place of humble submission. Jesus being in a conundrum, knowing that His purpose was to reach the lost sheep of Israel, but unable to say 'no' to Rebecca, decided to remain silent. His compassion tugging one way and His purpose tugging another must have been very difficult for Him. The decision to kneel before Him was the deciding factor that Jesus could not push past any longer. He looked at her, I imagine, with all the compassion a Savior would have and denied her request. "... It is not right to take the children's bread and throw it to the dogs." Matthew 15:26. Reading this statement, I thought to myself, "Really Jesus?" This woman is pouring out her heart and soul to You and this is the response you give her? The character of Jesus tells us there must be more to what He was saying. After thorough research, what Jesus was telling her was that it would be wrong to feed the family pet before feeding the children. Why is this important? Jesus is not denying that she belongs to the family, it is just not her turn yet. Unlike a stray, a pet is loved by the master. A pet has a home. A pet is taken care of. A pet *is* family.

Not Offended, Determined

Jesus had come with a distinct purpose to save the Jews. I would have taken offense to being compared to an animal at any length. Rebecca, however, was not. Her response was priceless as she continued to plead for her daughter. She was willing to accept any part of the meal she could get. "Yes, Lord, yet even the dogs eat the crumbs that fall from their masters' table." Whether Rebecca knew Old Testament scripture or not, she spoke to Jesus what had been written about Abraham and the extended blessings promised to the Gentiles, "...in you all the families of the earth will be blessed," Genesis 12:3. The disciples, having memorized Old Testament scripture, would have known what she was referring to. I can see them and Jesus, eyes big with amazement, thinking "What, did she just speak from the Pentateuch?" Jesus, extremely impressed by this woman's tenacity in her expression of faith, said to her, "O woman, great is your faith! Be it done for you as you desire." Rebecca's daughter received her healing instantly.

Tenacious Faith

This woman's tenacious faith in the healing ability of Jesus so impresses Him that He granted her wishes even though it conflicted with His purpose. How much more will Jesus grant us, those who belong to the body of Christ, our desires? Are you going to God in the righteous name of Jesus with your request? Or do you feel that there is some requirement you must fulfill before your submission? I often feel like there are some requirements before asking God for anything. For example, if I need something from God but I have not been in communication with Him all day or in a couple of days, I feel guilty asking. Let's think about that for a minute. Would we want our children to feel guilty or ashamed to come to us to ask for help if they have not told us they loved us today or in a couple of days? No. We want them to come to us with their needs, no matter what. We love them for who they are, not what they have or have not done. It is the same with God. Yes, God wants us to be more intentional about being in touch with

Him, but He does not withhold His love when we don't. He does not hold grudges against us if we don't. Do be intentional to spend time with God regularly, but don't withhold your request if you have not.

Our prayers may be awkward. Our attempts may be feeble. But since the power of prayer is in the hands of the One who hears it and not in the one who says it, our prayers do make a difference.

Max Lucado

Reflection Questions

1. Even Jesus took time to get away from the hustle and bustle to rest and refresh. How can you ensure that you are getting an ample amount of rest so that you can refresh? This could be doing simple things, such as taking a bath. It could also be on a larger scale, such as going on a trip.

2. When you put out a call for help to Jesus, what names do you use to call Him? Is it Father, Master, Protector, etc.? What is it about these names or particular attributes that affect you?

3. Describe a time when you felt like you were being ignored by God. What emotions did you experience, i.e., anger, resentment, impatience, etc.? How can you ensure the next time God is silent, you will react differently?

4. The disciples did not show the woman empathy or compassion. If you were in their shoes, do you believe you would have acted differently? Why or why not?

____

____

____

____

5. This woman gave every part of her being to get the attention of Jesus for the sake of her daughter. Have there been situations in your life that have caused you to cry out from the depths of your soul to reach Jesus? If so, how did it increase your faith?

____

____

____

____

CHAPTER 3

Not Enough to Share

But she said, "As the Lord your God lives, I don't have
anything baked – only a handful of flour in the jar and
a bit of oil in the jug. Just now, I am gathering a
couple of sticks in order to go prepare it for myself
and my son so that we can eat it and die."
1 Kings 17:12

This is a beautiful occurrence of obedience despite hopelessness. It begins when Elijah tells the king of Israel, Ahab, that there will be no rain for several years. King Ahab and his wife Jezebel had led the Israelites astray. Elijah, informing the king that there would be no rain meant that their food, finances, and health, would drastically be affected by their disobedience. How were they disobedient? I'm glad you asked. King Ahab married Jezebel who was from another nation and worshipped other gods. The Israelites were warned against intermingling with other nations because they would be led away from God and into idol worship. So, it was the union between Ahab and Jezebel that led them into worshipping idols. One of the idols they worshipped was Baal who they believed controlled the rain. God was about to remind them that He is the One and Only true God and that He is sovereign over all creation.

The Israelites were worshipping the gods of the other nations which God had vehemently prohibited. He told the Israelite nation in Deuteronomy 6:14-15, "Do not follow other gods, the gods of the peoples around you, for the Lord your God who is among you, is a jealous God." As a result of their disobedience, the Israelites would experience judgment. How fitting this story is for the 21st century as we chase after the gods of wealth, power, and prestige. They consume us to the point that we have no time for the God of the Universe, the God of creation, the God who provides the sun and the resources we use to live. What does it say about us who have a reference point in these Bible stories that God has provided us, and yet we make the same mistakes they did? The Israelites were still trying to get to know God. Who He was and what He required of them. We have a whole book to turn to for guidance, they did not. It has been many centuries later and we have not learned from the lessons past. We do the same thing they did, engage in idolatry. Our modern idols look a little different, but it is still the same behavior. The Israelites and Gentiles, Saints, and Sinners; same people, different time.

During the drought, God made provision for Elijah. He kept him hidden and safe. After Elijah made the declaration that the drought would take place for several years, God gave him specific instructions. He told Elijah in 1 Kings 17:2-3, "... Depart from here turn eastward and hide yourself by the brook Cherith which is east of the Jordan." God told Elijah that a raven would feed him day and night and he would be refreshed by the water from the brook. During times when life deals us hardship and we feel like we are in a drought, God will always provide a place where we can be hidden and safe. When my grief had completely overwhelmed me and I could not see my way out, I hid myself in God's word where he embraced me and let me cry and weep. The scripture that provided and continues to provide me the nourishment and comfort I need is 2 Corinthians 1:3-4, "Blessed be the God and Father of our Lord Jesus Christ, the Father of mercies and the God of all comfort, who comforts us in all our affliction, so that we may be able to comfort those who are in any affliction, with the comfort for which we ourselves are comforted by God." My grief is my drought and God's word is my provision. I am hidden and safe even when it doesn't feel that way.

Obedience Allows for Divine Provision

Elijah did not hesitate, ask questions, or doubt the word of the Lord. He immediately obeyed the instructions given to him. "So, he went and did according to the word of the Lord", 1 Kings 17:5. Elijah did not just go, he remained by the brook until the Lord gave him new instructions. There have been so many times when God has told me to go and do and I went and did, but instead of remaining content in where I was and what He told me to do, I became anxious. I started to wonder if I should be doing something else, or if I had been in that particular place long enough. Sometimes the people in our lives will make us feel like what we are doing is not enough. When I was working towards my degree, people would ask me, "What are your plans after graduation?" I really didn't know but felt like I should, which made me feel like something was wrong and I wasn't doing something right. I felt like the Lord led me to this particular course of action, but I allowed people to make me think there was more I should be doing. Once I graduated, people would ask, "So what are you going to do now?" I still didn't know. I knew the Lord opened doors for me to pursue this particular field, but He had not revealed to me exactly what I should do moving forward. I had to be honest and transparent. I just began to tell people that I was waiting on God. I am no longer worried about what's next because He has a plan for my life to serve others and bring Him glory. I just don't know exactly what that is yet. I will continue to work my nine to five until the plan becomes clear and I will be content in what I am currently doing. Notice I said *will* be content. Until now, writing these words, I understood this with my head, but not my heart. I trust God, and Elijah is showing me just how to do it. One second, one minute, one hour, one day at a time.

Elijah did not complain or pester God about what would happen if the brook dried up or if the raven stopped bringing him meat. He didn't need to worry or wonder because he knew God would provide and that is just what He did. "And after a while the brook dried up, because there was no rain in the land," 1 Kings 17:7. Elijah must have seen the brook getting lower and lower to the point where the brook became muddy sludge with undrinkable parts, and only a small area left from which to drink. I can feel my heart rate increase just thinking about being in his shoes, knowing the very thing that has kept him was almost depleted. Let's talk about the dried-up brook in our lives. The brook that once provided us sustenance, enjoyment, laughter, comfort, or security. The brook is the thing we go to when we need a boost, or an escape from life's demands, struggles, uncertainties, or pain. We all have a brook. There comes a time when the brook doesn't provide what it always did. Some brook examples are eating comfort food, consuming drugs, or alcohol, having sex, binge-watching TV, and working long hours to stay busy. These are all brooks that only provide temporary relief. When the brook dries up, the fulfillment that you used to receive has lost its luster and you are left feeling empty.

I spoke about grieving the loss of my dog Gracie. Losing her put me in a headspace where there was no amount of anything I could ingest from the outside that would remove the intense pain in my heart. Because I loved her so much, I did not want to numb with anything. I wanted to feel the loss because I felt that it was the only way I could feel her. I learned through this grieving process that when I numbed the bad, I also numbed the good. When I used different coping mechanisms to avoid times of pain and discomfort, I was also avoiding times of joy, laughter, and fun. I spent most of my life anesthetized, void of all emotion. Yes, I was there, and I was laughing and engaging, but it was a mask. Yes, I was listening, but I could not hear. I was asleep mentally for such a long time that I did not know what it meant to be fully awake and present. As I continued to grieve, I woke up in pain and went to bed in pain. I cried out to God from a place inside of me that I did not know existed. My brook had dried up and it was time for me to move into the next phase of my journey, just like Elijah.

A Divine Appointment

God had already prepared the next steps in Elijah's journey. He gave Elijah another set of specific instructions, "Arise, go to Zarephath, which belongs to Sidon, and dwell there. Behold, I have commanded a widow woman to feed you," 1 Kings 17:9. Zarephath, a widow, what? Elijah again does not hesitate, "So he arose and went to Zarephath ..." 1

Kings 17:10. First, Zarephath is the hometown of Jezebel, Ahab's wife. Why is this important? The region of Sidon is what would be considered the Baal belt. Baal was the false god that Ahab and Jezebel had encouraged the people of Israel to worship. In addition, Jezebel was assassinating God's true prophets. Secondly, how would a widow provide for Elijah? In those days, a widow was an outcast. Without a husband, she had no means to care for herself or her children unless she had some type of occupation, such as a midwife or prostitute. The Sidonian nation was ruled by Jezebel's father, and it is there that Baal worship originated. Why would God tell Elijah to live in the very place where Baal worship was a normal practice? God would use this very event to show the stark contrast between Israel's lack of faith and the expression of faith from a gentile woman. In addition, priests, which Elijah was, were supposed to be provided for by the Israelite nation according to Jewish law. Instead, Elijah would receive provision from a gentile, idol-worshipping woman.

Elijah exhibits faith in action. He immediately follows God's instructions. "So he arose and went to Zarephath …" 1 King 17:10. Zarephath was a day's journey, which meant Elijah was going on a mountainous journey with no food and no water. This speaks to his self-discipline and determination. I have a hard time fasting for eight hours sitting at home. Elijah's faith in God was not in vain. "And when he came to the gate of the city, behold, a widow was there…" 1 Kings 17:10. God's sovereignty is illuminated in this meeting between prophet and widow. Elijah didn't have to go looking for the woman ordained to feed him. God's timing was perfect. He arranged for the woman to have reached the end of her rope at just the right time for her to head out to prepare for her and her son's last meal. She stepped out into the vicinity of the city's gate right around the time Elijah would end his 24-hour journey. Elijah's trust in God was demonstrated in the fact that he did not wonder if this was the widow woman God told him about, he knew it was. She was not aware that her life was about to change, but Elijah did. Her obedience and faith would save Elijah, her son, and herself from death.

Hope in a Hopeless Situation

The widow, let's call her Paula, looked at the last of the flour and oil in her kitchen, and the hope that she had been holding onto for months vanished. She had prayed to her gods, and they had failed her. She looked at her son, who was skinny now from their food rationing due to the drought that had lasted way too long, and thought, we are going to die. I have failed him. It is in this state that she walks out to the city gate to gather sticks to cook their last meal and meets Elijah. "And he called to her and said, … Bring me a little water in a vessel, that I may drink," 1 Kings 17:10. Because God had prepared her heart to receive Elijah, she took her mind off her son long enough to help this strange man she recognized as a Jew. It could have been his accent or his attire that revealed his ethnicity. She agreed to get him water, but on her way to oblige him, he asked for something she did not have to give. "… Bring me a morsel of bread in your hand," 1 Kings 17:11. She thought to herself, now wait a minute. You have asked me for water which is in short supply but now you want the very thing of which I already don't have enough? She says to Elijah, "As the Lord your God lives, I have nothing baked, only a handful of flour in a jar and a little oil in a jug …" 1 Kings 17:12. In other words, I swear to you that I don't have enough for you. I have just enough for me and my boy, and I choose us. She spoke from her lack first in response to his request and concluded with her hopelessness. "… And now I am gathering a couple of sticks that I may go in and prepare it for myself and my son, that we may eat it and die," 1 Kings 17:12. There is a difference between fact and truth. The fact of the matter was that she did not have enough flour or oil. The truth is that God is more than enough, and He will provide. A fact is when it rains outside you will get wet. The truth is, you can walk out into the rain and not get wet if you have an umbrella. Elijah had an umbrella for Paula, she just had to open it.

Elijah sensing her fear and hearing the apprehension in her voice said, "Do not fear…" 1 Kings 17:13. How could she not be afraid? She was down to her very last, and she was dependent on it to feed herself and her son one more time. Paula was afraid before she saw Elijah and now more so because he wanted the very last of her security. Elijah reassured her, "For thus says the Lord, the God of Israel, 'The jar of flour shall not be spent, and the jug of oil shall not be empty, until the day that the Lord sends rain upon the earth,'" 1 Kings 17:14. I am sure she had heard about the God of the Israelites and all that He had done on their behalf. I can imagine Paula thinking, will your God really come through for me and my boy? If I trust this odd-looking man, I have more to gain than I have to lose. I only have one more day of supplies left but what if I can have more? She decided to take a chance and have faith in the God of Israel. "And she went and did as Elijah had said...," 1 Kings 17:15.

There are times in our lives when our situation has been hopeless, it's the last dollar and not enough to get gas to make it to work, we've talked until we are blue in the face and the wayward child or the failing marriage does not improve, or we've studied all we can for the test and still feel lost. We have done all we can do, and we finally just let go. It is in those very times that God will step in and do what we can't. He gives us the peace to move forward regardless of the circumstances. Sometimes it will go the way we desire and sometimes it will not. God knows best and sometimes what we want is not His best for us. It is in these times when we must lean in, and on Him and trust His plan. Jeremiah 29:11-12 says, "For I know the plans I have for you, declares the Lord, plans for welfare and not for evil, to give you a future and a hope. You will seek me and find me, when you seek me with all your heart."

When my children were little, I lived in this apartment that I could not afford. It would cost more than one bi-monthly paycheck so I would have to split the rent between two pay periods. This strategy was very ineffective and got me further and further in the hole. It would cause me to be late on the rent which cost me a huge late fee. At the time I was not tithing but one day felt convicted about it. All I could think was, "How am I supposed to give tithe from my lack?" I already didn't have enough. Matthew 3:10 says, "Bring the whole tithe into the storehouse, that there may be food in my house. Test me in this ... and see if I will not throw open the floodgates of heaven and pour out so much blessing that there will not be room enough to store it." I tested God and began to tithe. My household never went without. We always had food, clothes, and a roof over our heads. Some of the things I wanted I didn't always have but I had everything I needed.

Before I knew it, I was moving out into a nicer apartment that cost much less and had more space. Because of this faith experience, I make it a point to give tithe, not because I want something in return but because I appreciate all that God does for me and my family.

It is when we surrender, when we actually let go of doing it our way and look to Him to show us the way. When we do, He looks at us as we would a little boy or girl. He cleans us up, picks us up, and makes everything better. That is what He did for Paula. He looked at her with compassion, even though she was not looking at Him. He saw her and fulfilled her needs. It makes me wonder, was she being used to provide for Elijah, or was Elijah being used to provide for her? Maybe it was both. Either way, God received the glory from a *former* idol-worshipping woman. Why do I say former? Well, it is because God proved Himself to her. "... And she and her household ate for many days. The jar of flour was not spent, neither did the jug of oil become empty, according to the word of the LORD that he spoke by Elijah," 1 Kings 17:15-16. He proved there is no one greater than Him. She had called on the gods of her people and no help had come. But when she believed and obeyed the God of Israel, He revealed Himself to her and rewarded her faith with the miracle she needed.

Reflection Questions

1. Elijah had a lot of courage. When was there a time in your life when God instructed you to do something that could have put you in harm's way? How did you respond to His request?

2. In what ways did Elijah express his faith in God? Provide some examples when the expression of your faith was impactful.

3. How would you have responded if Elijah requested your last meal meant for you and your children?

4. How did the widow woman's obedience impact her and her son's life?

5. We often discount our abilities, gifts, or talents, seeing them as insignificant. God
   has blessed each of us with gifts. Reflect on what you have that can be used to
   bless the people of God.

____

____

____

____

*May the God of Hope fill you
with all joy and peace in
believing, so that by the
power of the Holy Spirit you
may abound in hope.*

Romans 15:13

CHAPTER 4

Not Too Few

"When the vessels were full, she said to her son,
"Bring me another vessel." And he said to her, "There
is not another." Then the oil stopped flowing."
2 Kings 4:6

Here is an account of a widow who is grieving and in jeopardy of losing her children. She receives the compassion of God through the prophet Elisha. Elisha was discipled by the mighty Elijah, and he took over as mentor and teacher at the School of the Prophets. This wonderful miraculous encounter with Elisha and the widow shows us how God hears each of His children and how He shows up to answer our call. We will see the desperate circumstances this widow woman is facing, how she obediently responds to the man of God, and how God shows His mighty hand of grace and kindness towards her.

This unnamed widow woman, we will call her Liberty, has lost her husband. He has died and left her and their two sons with his debt. It is being sought after by the creditor. To most of us today, this is not a big deal since there are a great deal of people in debt. In the 21st century, the result of unpaid debt may be a negative mark on our credit report giving us a low credit score. The worst-case scenario would be to have our wages garnished or our property confiscated. For Liberty, the unpaid debt comes at a much higher cost. In ancient Israel, not only could your property be taken, but you and or your children could be enslaved to pay off the debt. In Liberty's case, the creditor was coming for her children. The thought of losing my property or having my wages garnished is devastating, but taking my children is altogether unthinkable. Liberty must have been out of her mind, completely distraught, and consumed with worry. According to Jewish law, the creditor could only enslave someone who owed them money for a limited time and the slaves were supposed to be treated as hired workers. Some creditors were enslaving debtors indefinitely and enforcing hard labor on them. This is what Liberty was facing and, in her desperation, she reached out to the man of God, the mighty prophet Elisha for help.

Liberty not knowing what else to do cries out to Elisha. "Your servant my husband is dead, and you know that your servant feared the Lord, but the creditor has come to take my two children to be his slaves," 2 Kings 4:1. Liberty cried out in distress, fear, and helplessness. She was in an economic, familial, emotional, and spiritual crisis. Her only hope was to reach God and she would do that through His prophet. Liberty first establishes her right to address Elisha. Her statement, *"Your servant my husband"* tells us that she is letting Elisha know that she is justified in coming to him for help. She is not a random woman coming to him because he is a prophet. Liberty points out that her husband was his servant. Elisha knew her husband, and probably very well. She then, speaks of her husband's character. *"... you know that your servant feared the Lord ..."* In this context, her husband was not afraid of the Lord but revered and honored God. For her to make this statement means he had to be a righteous man. Jesus had not yet descended to the earth in human form, so works were required to be considered righteous. With that in mind, this means he was an upright man, he took care of the things of God, and his family, and was honest. This makes sense because her next statement expresses her discontent. *"... but the creditor has come to take my two children to be his slaves ..."* In other words, my husband has served you and the Lord. His sacrifice and service should mean something. Why is God allowing creditors to take my sons? Her husband, even though he had a family, must have spent a considerable amount of time at the School of the Prophets, leaving his wife and family to fend for themselves. Liberty missed out on time with her husband because of his calling and development with the other prophets. He died, leaving her physically to take care of herself and her sons. And her sons, who are now her lifeline since she is a widow, are in danger of being taken from her. Even though her husband served Elisha, he was a good husband, and feared the Lord, the creditor was still coming to take her children. In this culture, a woman remained with her family until given away in marriage. This means Liberty is used to relying on others for provision. God was getting ready to show her that He was the **source** and those who had provided for her up to this point were the **resource**.

The Complaint

Liberty looked at her circumstances and accused Elisha and God of not caring. Isn't that what we do? When things don't look or seem the way we want them to, we blame God and ask Him why. When Gracie was killed, that was my first question, why? I had such a short time with her, and she was just a baby. I was so hurt. I could not breathe, I could not eat, I could not think about anything else but the circumstances of the day when she died. I was consumed with grief. I longed to pet, hug, and love on her. I yearned for her. At times for a few seconds, I would forget that she was gone and look for her and relive the tragedy all over again. This went on for weeks, and the entire time I was asking God why and I was accusing Him of not caring about my pain. Saying things like, "Aren't You the Most-High God that sees the end from the beginning?" and "Aren't You the One who holds the world in your hand?" I didn't realize that God allowed the pain, doubt, distress, grief, anger, and blame so that I could mature. He allowed it so that I could see that even though I was in a bad place, He was there with me. Through this entire process, the testing of my faith, all I could do in between blaming, accusing, and being angry was say "God help me." I would cry out often because it was all I knew to do. I knew He was THE *ONLY* one who could help me. I knew I needed Him. Liberty was in the same position I was, only God could help her. Although she was accusatory, she still turned to the man of God for help. It is because of our pain that we are drawn to our knees to the God of mercy and comfort. His open arms lead us into a new, deeper relationship with Him. Each trial of life takes us to a new level in our maturity and faith journey.

The Response

Elijah's response to Liberty's cries was nothing less than pure compassion. He did not ignore or send her away. He gave her his full attention and support. Elisha asked her "What can I do for you?" 2 Kings 4:2. This question must have given her some relief. In essence, he was asking, how can I help you? I can imagine the bewildered look on Liberty's face. His care and concern must have shocked her. I can see him taking her hands and looking at her with love and attentiveness. She asked for help, and he immediately jumped in and offered his assistance. She may have gone to him hoping to get help but in her head thinking she was going to have to beg and plead. But what Elijah exhibited was probably the same tenacity in serving her as her husband did in serving him. He was eager to help her. His eagerness is seen in the double question posed to her. Elisha was a prophet who could hear from God. The Holy Spirit leads him to ask about what is in her home. There is a resource she has that will sustain and keep her. He asked, "What can I do for you?" and then asked, "... what do you have in the house?" 2 Kings 4:2. She has discounted the little she has as insignificant just like the Widow of Zarephath. She stated, "Your servant has nothing in the house except a jar of oil," 2 Kings 4:2. When we bring what we have to God, He multiplies it. When we start a statement with, "I only" or "I am just", we are limiting the God on the inside of us. In many cases, oil represents the Spirit of God. Liberty was sad, distressed, and hopeless. I can see Elisha smiling at her thinking, that even a little is much with God. Liberty did not sit home and cry. She did not run to her friends and complain about her woes. She did not use this pain and distress as an excuse to turn on God. She knew that she could go to the Prophet who would reach God on her behalf. Today, we don't need a human mediator between us and God because Jesus' death and resurrection allow us the right to go to the throne of God on our own behalf to receive mercy and find grace, Hebrews 4:16.

Liberty went to the man of God for a solution to her dire circumstances. Her situation was critical, and her needs required urgent relief. She was about to lose her boys. She must have been terrified and frantic. The fear and panic were all over her as she paced when telling her story to Elisha. There was no arrogance and matter of fact about her approach. Her posture was imploring and persuasive as she cried out to Elisha. He grabbed her attention, "I can help you, what do you have in your house?" "Huh," was her response. She was thinking, if I had something in my house that would help me, I wouldn't need to come to you for help. But, she said, "… nothing in the house except a jar of oil." Elisha told her "Go outside, borrow vessels from all your neighbors, empty vessels and not too few …" 2 Kings 4:3. Liberty listened intently to the instructions of Elisha. She must have been thinking, "empty vessels, why wouldn't I get full vessels?" God would show her that He is the source of all our resources. We must rely not on the resources but on the one who provides them. If she received full vessels from her neighbors, this would only create more debt for her that she would be expected to pay back. God's gifts are without repentance. What God gives you will not be taken back. In our emptiness, God can fill us with more of Himself. God had removed all the things and people she had become dependent upon, leaving her disheveled and empty. This emptiness, and not having anything, or anyone is what forced her to come to God. Now she can see what she did not see before her husband died and left her in a dreadful situation. God is more than the sum total of her resources. With open eyes, she can begin a new relationship and journey with the True and Living God.

The Overflow

Liberty immediately obeyed Elisha. She was beginning to have some hope but, probably still doubting a bit too. This is the human response. The fence. Hoping it is true or will happen, but not wanting to put so much faith in it that it crushes us if it is not successful. "So she went from him and shut the door behind herself and her sons. And as she poured, they brought the vessels to her," 2 Kings 4:5. She went to all her neighbors asking to borrow their empty vessels. Her neighbors and friends would readily lend vessels that were empty as they would have no value. To Liberty, they had **great value** because, based on Elisha, she was going to fill them up. Elisha told her, "… go in and shut the door behind yourself and your sons and pour into these vessels. And when one is full, set it aside," 1 Kings 4:5. We don't know how many vessels she was able to borrow but we do know that it was not a few. I find it interesting that Liberty had no idea what she was going to do with the vessels of oil, she was only doing as instructed, hoping for a miracle. Olive oil in the first century was very valuable because it had many purposes. It was used for cooking, anointing, fuel for oil lamps, soap-making, skincare, and medicine to name a few. Even though these uses were well known, Liberty still had no clue why she was filling vessels. I wonder what she was thinking as she poured the oil that she originally counted as insignificant into vessel after vessel. I imagine some vessels were small, but some may have been very large. "When the vessels were full, she said to her son, Bring me another vessel. And he said, there is not another. Then the oil stopped flowing," 2 Kings 4:6. Liberty has not too few vessels full of oil and the oil she originally started with. I can see her looking at the full vessels while holding the little jar of oil in her hand. She is amazed, flustered, and amused at the same time, thinking, how can this be? How can something so small fill up so many vessels? That, Ms. Liberty, is the power, love, and mercy of God. Yes, your husband was a servant of God, and yes, he feared the Lord. But it is even better than that. You are His beloved daughter, and He is your provider. I say to you, the one reading this book, as well as myself, you are His child and He is the Source of all your resources, and He loves you and will provide for you. Fear not, for I am with you; be not dismayed, for I am your God; I will strengthen you, I will help you, I will uphold you with my righteous right hand," Isaiah 41:10.

The Redemption

Liberty returns to the man of God with pep in her step. This time she comes not out of despair, frustration, defeat, and anger but of enlightenment. She has seen the power of God through the work of her hands and in front of her own eyes. This is not a story that was told to her, she is a witness. She told Elisha with excitement; I filled all the vessels my neighbors loaned me with only my little jar of oil and the oil did not stop flowing until I ran out of vessels. She was no longer empty as a result of her husband's death and the threat of her sons being taken from her. Those things have not been changed, but she has seen the hand of God, and her focus has changed. If God can fill not too few vessels with the little jar of oil she had, He can most definitely help her resolve her issues. Her focus has moved from her problems to her God. The fear, respect, and honor she must now have for God whom she previously blamed for taking her husband and making her vulnerable to creditors to take her sons. She now understands her husband's passion for serving. So, she tells Elisha the wonderful thing she has just experienced at his direction and eagerly awaits his next set of instructions. Elisha tells her, "... Go, sell the oil and pay your debts, and you and your sons can live on the rest," 2 Kings 4:7. Not only does Liberty have enough to pay her debts, but she also has enough to provide for her and her boys for the rest of their lives. Wow, she must have collected quite a few vessels. There was so much oil that Liberty now has a lucrative business. She is now a business owner. The people she borrowed vessels from would now become her customers. Liberty thought the death of her husband was a thing to despise but it was his death that brought her life, and to know the True and Living God. It was extremely painful and scary for her when she lost her husband. He was her mate. He courted her, she loved him, and she shared children with him. And now because of his relationship with God and the prophet, she has been personally introduced to God and knows that it was not her husband that provided for them all the years they were together, but it was God. God will use our pain to bring us to Himself and show us what it really means to live a life of true abundance.

Reflection Questions

1. Liberty is distraught with worry and pain. What complaint and request
    does she bring to Elisha? Describe a time when you were disappointed in
    the way God handled a situation in your life. How did you respond?

2. What do you think Liberty was expecting Elisha to do to help her? Has
    there been a time when your need was so great you didn't know what to
    ask for? How did you express your need?

3. How did Elisha respond to her appeal for help? Was his reaction
    surprising to you? Why or why not?

4. Would you have had immediate obedience to Elisha's request to borrow
    vessels from neighbors like Liberty? Why do you think she quickly obeyed?

5. Her obedience resulted in a business that would provide for her family for years to come. Describe a time when a lack of or slow obedience to Christ caused you to miss an opportunity for a blessing.

____

____

____

____

God is our refuge and strength, always ready to help in times of trouble. So we will not fear when earthquakes come and mountains crumble into the sea. Let the oceans roar and foam. Let the mountains tremble as the waters surge.

Psalms 46:1-3

CHAPTER 5
Nope, I'm Good

Through Gehazi Elisha said, "You've gone far beyond the call of duty in taking care of us; what can we do for you? Do you have a request we can bring to the king or to the commander of the army?' She replied, "Nothing. I'm secure and satisfied in my family?" 2 Kings 4:13 (MSG)

Here we have another unnamed woman. She is only known as the Shunammite woman. We will call her Deborah. Deborah was a wealthy woman who lived in Shunem with her husband. She met Elisha the prophet in town as he was passing through on one of his journeys. They started a conversation, and she invited him to dinner. This began a ritual of visits to Deborah's home. In this story, Deborah shows Elisha hospitality and generosity expecting nothing in return. She saw that he was a man of God and wanted to honor him. Elisha was very grateful for her kindness and wanted to reward her. Although she denied that she needed anything, Elisha pressed his servant to find out what could be done for her. He eventually figures out her deepest desire and provides her with the very thing she had given up on receiving.

Tripping through Shunem

Elisha started out on his first of a series of trips through Shunem. As he walked through town, there was a wealthy woman who was out shopping. She was picking through the fresh apples, pears, and oranges when she noticed him. He stood out to her, and she thought, "I have never seen this man before. I wonder who he is." Elisha was walking through noticing all the activity in the town when Deborah walked up to him. She introduced herself and they began to talk. Elisha was a little taken aback by her forwardness, but she seemed nice enough.

Deborah was very intrigued by the things he spoke about. As she intently listened to Elisha, he thought to himself, "She has very kind and generous spirit." They talked for quite some time when suddenly Deborah got excited. She said, "Why don't you come over for dinner and meet my husband." It's getting late, come get a warm meal before continuing your journey," she said. He tried to refuse her, but she insisted. He thought about it and concluded that Deborah was a very nice woman who was genuine. What could it hurt for me to sit down and break bread with her and her husband (we will call him Joe)?

Keeping with Jewish custom, Elisha walks into an area of Deborah's home and a servant greets them to wash their feet and cleanse their hands. Joe comes out to meet the man his wife has brought home. He wonders what is it about this man that my wife found it necessary to bring him to our home. Once they all sat down to talk and eat, Joe was also intrigued with Elisha. He was different than anyone they have ever met. He talked about the miracles he had seen his mentor Elijah perform, and the ones he himself has performed. He spoke with boldness and kindness at the same time. His speech was elegant and inspiring. They all ate, laughed, and enjoyed each other's company well into the evening. After an enjoyable meal and great conversation, Elisha finally says his goodbyes and heads out to continue his journey.

Elisha began to regularly pass through Shunem. Each time he would stop by Joe and Deborah's home for a meal and catch up on the latest events and activities. Elisha talked about his journey and miracles. Deborah and Joe would talk about all the things going on in town and the latest news with friends and family. They would all be very engaged, asking each other thought-provoking questions about this and that. They had become fast friends. After every meal, Elisha would thank the lovely couple for their generosity and kindness and bless their home. He would then say his goodbyes until the next time he was passing through.

After some time of these visits from Elisha, Deborah stated to Joe, "I know this is a holy man of God," 2 Kings 4:9. Elisha was a kind and compassionate man, performing miracles to help others prosper and call out those who were doing wrong. Instead of taking the credit, he honored God for the things his hands performed. He was honest and generous, not asking for payment for his service, but helping from his heart. Deborah was so moved by Elisha's character, that she asked her husband if they could build onto their home to create space for him. She asked, "Please, let us make a small upper room on the wall; and let us put a bed for him there, and a table and a chair and a lampstand; so, it will be that whenever he comes to us, he can turn in there," 2 Kings 4:10. Family structures and homes in those times were very different than in our time. When families became larger, they did not move away. Instead, accommodations were made for the family to remain whole. When couples got married, quarters were built on top of the family home. This is what she was asking to do for Elisha.

Deborah no longer saw him as a traveling friend but as someone she would consider a part of their family. Not only this, she wanted to honor him as a man of God by suggesting they add not just a room but tools for him to continue his work. She wanted him to be comfortable. A bed would not be enough, but he would also need other furniture as well. He would need a bed to rest between his journey trips, a lampstand for which to put a candle to see at night, and a table and chair to study. This is taking generosity to the next level. She has gone beyond being courteous. She has moved from the kindness of a stranger to caring for him like a loved one. It was made known that whenever he would come their way, provision had been set aside for him. He would have a hot meal, company, and a place to rest and study. They would be his traveling family that would eagerly await his return every time he departed. It is wonderful to be embraced by people who don't want anything from you but your company. They weren't asking him to perform any miracles or do anything for them. They weren't even asking for payment for his stay at their home. They just wanted to serve him and enjoyed talking to him about his adventures.

It was a Set-up

Deborah, Joe, nor Elisha knew what God was doing. They had no idea that this meeting was a set-up. It was a divine appointment between the prophet and a woman's dream. God is so amazing in the way He works. He allowed this woman to give up on her deepest desire and then showed up at a time when she least expected it. She would never see it coming. She had just met the answer to her prayers and didn't know it. When God sent the prophet her way, she was moved with compassion. She had not allowed her unanswered prayer to make her bitter. So, when she saw this man, it was not a burden to show him kindness.

When I met Gracie on that walking path, I had no idea how she would impact my life. All I knew was there was this little puppy alone and afraid. I was compelled with compassion to help her. I could not walk by and leave her there. It was the end of November and freezing. My heart went out to her, and I had to help. Our meeting was at a time when I had relapsed into smoking marijuana and drinking alcohol again. I knew this way of life was not God's best for me. I knew God wanted to use me, but I had a problem, *AND* I loved God. Let's put a pin here for a moment. We have to stop condemning people for their journey. Just because people are not at their best and may be in bondage, does not mean they don't love God, or don't desire better for themselves. I deeply wanted to be used by Him and to do His will, but I was so weak. I kept getting delivered and going back to the very thing I was delivered from. Just like the Israelites in the book of Judges. They would fall into idolatry, God would allow them to be captured by their enemies, they would cry out for mercy and deliverance, and God would redeem them by placing a righteous judge over them. The new judge was vital in turning their hearts back to God and helping them govern their lives after God. However, once the judge died, they would fall back into idolatry and start the cycle all over again. That was me, over and over again. Then, I met Gracie. It was a set-up. My life did not change while she lived but when she died, it started an awakening in me. It was a long-drawn-out process of grief, despair, anger, and frustration, BUT God. It was through my pain that God broke the cycle.

God set up this connection to start my deliverance process that would take me exactly where He wanted me and where I had been trying to get. Now, I can see clearly, and my sight is no longer blurry. I can hear, and my ears are no longer dull. I can feel, and I am not bogged down by unaddressed sin and grief. Pain will allow God to perform surgery, taking us through the healing process, and put us in place to receive what we've been asking for and what He wants for us. And most of the time when He does it, we won't see it coming. Deborah's hospitality shocked Elisha and because she was so persistent, he couldn't refuse her. She did not know why she was so compelled to bring this man to her home, she just knew she must. Elisha had no idea how much she would bless him. He just saw a very insistent woman and felt welcomed by her kindness.

Deborah chose to be kind to Elisha. She had an open heart and she allowed him into it. I think about the friendships I have had throughout my life. Each friendship was deliberately chosen. There was something about each person that I was drawn to and desired to be around. Family is chosen for you, but we choose our friends. These relationships can form bonds sometimes stronger than blood relationships simply because of choice. I think about how friendships are formed. One friendship I had started in turmoil and fighting. We ended up as friends for a large part of my childhood. We were inseparable and we were nothing alike. She was bold and I was timid, she lived a religious lifestyle, and in my home, we did not. I was attracted to her and her family. Their family truly cared for each other and enjoyed being together. I desired that. She had a mom and dad who loved each other and that was something foreign to me. Even in our differences I loved her and wanted to spend as much time with her as I could. I'm sure Deborah and Joe felt the same way about Elisha. They were very different, but they cared for each other, appreciated those differences, and enjoyed being in each other's company. I had another friend that I met in my early 20s. Our friendship lasted into my late 30s. We were also very different, even in appearance. She is tall and I am short, she was very confident, and I was not, and she had a great work ethic, and I definitely did not. She challenged me to be better physically, mentally, and professionally. She was not afraid to tell me when I was wrong or when I needed to make some changes in my life. She did not condemn me but did evaluate my choices and challenged me to change. At the time it would annoy me when she was telling me about myself. In most cases she was right, and I had to admit it. I learned to appreciate her advice and observations because I knew she loved me and wanted me to make better choices so that I could have a better life.

As people, we are made to be in community. As much as some of us feel we don't need anyone and would rather be alone, that is a false narrative being played in our minds. We were created to socialize and gather together. People need people. Jesus is a prime example of this. When He walked the earth, He chose 12 men and a few women to walk alongside Him on His journey to preach about the Kingdom of God. It is important that we realize and accept that alone we cannot make it. We need each other.

> *Two people are better off than one, for they can help each other succeed. If one person falls, the other can reach out and help. But someone who falls alone is in real trouble. Likewise, two people lying close together can keep each other warm. But how can one be warm alone? A person standing alone can be attacked and defeated, but two can stand back-to-back and conquer. Three are even better, for a triple-braided cord is not easily broken. (Ecclesiastes 4:9-16)*

Generosity is Felt

Joe and Deborah built the room on top of their home so that Elisha would be more comfortable. I wonder if they decided to surprise him or if the work was completed before his next visit. Either way, one day he came along with his attendant to visit. This time, he did not have to leave for other accommodations after dinner because his friends had made provision for him. He stayed at his friend's home in the room that was specially made for him. What a blessing that is.

Elisha walked into what was now his room. Immediately looking forward, he noticed there was a small table positioned in front of a window. It had writing material placed neatly on top of it. A chair sat in front of the table. Looking to his right, he saw a bed with a pillow on it that looked very inviting. Beside the bed was a lampstand with an oil lamp for light already filled with oil. He was so impressed at the length to which that had went to make him feel at home. He had someone who had no blood relation to him care about him so much that they incurred an expense just so that he could remain with them and be comfortable. They gifted him with love without cost. Isn't that what Jesus has done for us? He gifted Himself to us with no request for payment. He knew the cost was too high for us. So, He said, "No worries, I got you. I'm going to pay this debt for you. Since I am the Son of the One you owe, it will be paid in full. Your debt has been wiped clean." With the gift of Jesus' life, He restored us back into relationship with God. Joe and Deborah freely and genuinely loved Elisha and they honored him not just with what they said but with action. People are quick to utter the words "I love you." However, we must see love as not just an emotion. Love causes us to act. Love causes us to be selfless. Love causes us to be inconvenienced. Love causes us to get uncomfortable and vulnerable. Love causes us to look beyond ourselves. That is why without God, we don't know love. He had to show us what it was. It is not what the world has shown us. Love came in human flesh and gave His life so that we could live for eternity.

Love is patient and kind. Love is not jealous or boastful or proud or rude.
It does not demand its own way. It is not irritable, and it keeps no record
of being wronged. It does not rejoice about injustice but rejoices
whenever the truth wins out. Love never gives up, never loses faith, is
always hopeful, and endures through every circumstance. (1 Corinthians
4:4-7)

Elisha was so grateful for the kindness of his new friends that he was overtaken with a desire to thank them and show his gratitude. He asked his servant to call Deborah. He wanted to let her know how indebted he felt. "He ordered his attendant Gehazi, call this Shunammite woman. So, he called her, and she stood before him," 2 Kings 4:12. He wanted her to know that what they did for him was so unexpected and remarkable that he needed to do something for the couple. "Then he said to Gehazi, "Say to her, 'Look you've gone to all this trouble for us. What can we do for you? Can we speak on your behalf to the king or to the commander of the army?" 2 Kings 4:13. Interestingly, he called Deborah, not Joe. As a prophet, it may have been revealed to him that she was the one who suggested they serve him with this gift. Or it could be the introduction in the marketplace that drew him into their lives and caused him to call her instead of Joe. In any case, he wanted her to understand that he was in a position to help her in any way she needed. Although she was not looking for him to repay her or give her accolades, it must have been very pleasing for her that he offered.

We all need something. There is an unspoken desire we all have. Something that even as a kid we may have dreamed about that has not taken its course. We may have given up on the dream or desire thinking it will never take place. Thinking the dream was too big and out of reach, we let the dream or idea die. Elisha was God's prophet, a man to whom God revealed secret things and who could see past the surface into the deep things. God had not revealed to him exactly what it was Deborah needed or wanted but he knew there was something there behind her kind eyes. Behind her humility, there was a gut-level desire that she had left in the posterior of her mind and heart. She had been disappointed so many times that she thought not to offer or speak about this desire ever again. Not to her husband, her friends, or even this prophet whom she respected and honored.

Deborah, not wanting Elisha to know her deepest desires or having them tucked away so tightly she never thought to bring them up to him. She replied, "... I live among my own people," 2 Kings 4:13. The Message version says, "Nothing, I'm secure and satisfied in my family." Not to be undone, Elisha asked his attendant, "Then what shall be done for her?" 2 Kings 4:14. The question is not about what can be done for them but what can be done for *her*. This is intriguing to me because in whatever way he blesses Deborah, it will be a blessing for both her and Joe. This tells me that this divine set-up is specifically for Deborah. God saw her and knew her. He waited until she had completely let go and given up on her dream. It was His time to shine. His time to bring the dream to pass and he was using her kindness and Elisha's desire to show his gratitude to do it. God would get the glory, no one else. He does the same thing for you and me. When He responds to our prayer it will come in a way that we know it was only God that could have pulled it off.

I had been praying for God to move me out of my current role so that I can use my degree that I worked so hard for. I had a speaking engagement with a church and thought surely this is what He wanted me to do. I was promised I would be contacted for other speaking engagements, but I never heard back from the organizer. It was a little disappointing, but I know how God works, so I let it go. My boss connected me with some friends in high places at the organization I work for, and it also sounded promising. The lady she introduced me to was very eager to use the talents I gained from my education. However, what she wanted to use me for was not effective or impactful. Another disappointment. Then God spoke to me and told me, "What I will give you, it will be unmistakable that it is from me. It will not come any other way and I will receive the glory." After that, I relaxed and settled in where I was until the day He would open a door or pave a way for me.

What was this desire that Deborah had kept hidden, tucked away in the recesses of her heart to never be seen or heard of by anyone? I'm glad you asked. Gehazi replies to Elisha, "... she has no son, and her husband is old." 2 Kings 4:14. He did not say *they* were old, which could imply that Deborah was still of childbearing age. She was barren and unable to conceive. I can imagine the disappointment each month when her time had come, and she realized yet again she had not conceived. I can understand her disappointment. Hoping this is the time and then it isn't. Building up the excitement to be let down, time and time again. In the first century, a woman's primary role was to bear children. Just like Hannah, she must have had a myriad of emotions. Fear, as her husband had every right to divorce her. Discouragement, as I am sure she continually prayed for God to give her children. Guilt, as she may have thought she had done something to cause God to punish her. Deborah was about to receive information that would change her life and cause her to have another myriad of emotions.

Blessings and Promises

Elisha now had information about Deborah that he knew must be a pain spot for her. He would be the instrument by which she would receive a blessing that could only come from God. He told Gehazi to call the Shunammite back. "... Call her. And when he called her, she stood in the doorway." 2 Kings 4:15. Deborah had returned to the task of cleaning up the dining area. She had just cleared off the table and was heading to the kitchen to clean their dishes and put food away when she heard Gehazi call her again. She hurried back up to the new room that had been built for Elisha wondering what could be the problem. She eagerly stood in the doorway waiting to hear what Elisha wanted. But what she heard almost crushed her. Elisha tells her "... about this time next year, you shall embrace a son..." 2 Kings 4:16. She gasps, her eyes widen, and she backs away from Elisha. There is so much pain that she can barely stand up. Her heart physically hurts because of the disappointment she has endured all these years. She does not want to believe, or hope, or even consider her dream would come to pass. All the emotions that flowed through her were felt in her statement to Elisha. "No, my lord, O man of God; do not lie to your servant." 2 Kings 4:16. She knew Elisha was a man of integrity and would not lie to her, but she did not want to believe the words he was saying to her. She wanted him to take them back. She did not want to feel the pain of hope and disappointment. She spent too many years with these awful feelings. When you are not hopeful, disappointment does not come. Now he was asking her to hope again. Her heart was saying no, no, no. I cannot do this again. Do not tell me to do this again.

She went back to the kitchen, but she was in a fog. She was in her own thoughts and could barely focus on cleaning the kitchen. She knew he was a prophet. Over the many visits he had with them, Elisha had told them many stories of the miracles he had performed and things that have come to pass because of his word. The problem was that this gift had been turned towards her. This would require her to have faith (hope) again. She had to believe that what he was saying would actually happen. Deborah said to herself, "I want to believe." She thought, "Can it be, that I will have a baby after all this time?" It was her time, and it would come to pass.

For the vision is for an appointed time; it testifies about the end and will not lie. Though it delays, wait for it, since it will certainly come and will not be late. (Habakkuk 2:3)

The promises of God are true. He is not a man that He can lie. What He told the prophet did in fact come to pass. "The woman conceived and gave birth to a son at the same time the following year, as Elisha had promised her." 2 Kings 4:17. It is amazing, that after all this time she actually held a child. Let's talk about what may have taken place within the time of a year. There are twelve months in a year, and it only takes nine months to term for a healthy baby. How long did Deborah have to wait? Was it two months, or three months? The torture she must have felt in month one when her time of the month came. She had to endure the anguish of the loss of something she had not been able to grasp her hands or mind around. She grieved the loss for another month because there was no baby. Month three, she said, "It must happen in order for the man of God's word to be fulfilled." Hope can be so agonizing and tiresome. But in month three, there was no blood, and her hope increased. She knew that she was with child as the end of the month approached and her time still had not come. Now, the agony of hope that she would carry to term. She kept telling herself, "He said she would hold a baby this time next year, so I must believe." Her time came, and the labor of the baby being burst from her womb arrived. As painful as childbirth is, she barely felt the pain as she anticipated holding the baby that she had waited decades to meet. She eagerly awaited Elisha's next visit. She may have believed he was a true prophet of God before, but now she had proof. She also knew without a shadow of a doubt that God sees her and loves her. The dreams we have are given to us by God Himself. He gives us a snapshot of what He wants for us by placing them in our hearts. Don't let go of the dream, hold on tight and believe that if He has given it to you, He will bring it to pass.

<u>Generosity</u>

The habit of giving freely without expecting anything in return.

Reflection Questions

1. Deborah had a heart of generosity shown through her insistence on Elisha coming to her home for dinner. In what ways do you show generosity to others?

____

____

____

____

2. What was it about Elisha do you think made her believe he was a man of God? Have you had people identify you as a follower of Christ? If so, what characteristics stood out to them?

____

____

____

____

3. How do you think Elisha felt when Deborah and Joe told him they had created space in their lives for him? Describe a time when you went out of your way for someone who least expected it.

____

____

____

____

4. Why do you think Deborah responded to Elisha the way she did when he told her she would conceive a child? How do you believe you would have responded if you were in her shoes?

____

____

____

5. Deborah's dream of having a child finally came to pass. What dreams have you given up on or forgotten about? Ask God to rekindle the faith to believe that dreams do come true. With God nothing is impossible.

____

____

____

____

CHAPTER 6
Not At All Concerned

"And standing behind him at his feet, weeping, she began to wet his feet with her tears and wiped them with the hair of her head and kissed his feet and anointed them with the ointment." Luke 7:38

In this story, we see what seems like a genuine offer to befriend Jesus. There are three people in this encounter with many watching. We have a Pharisee, Simon, who invites Jesus to dinner. Jesus who kindly accepts the offer to dine with Simon. And finally, the "Sinner Woman" who crashes dinner, we will call her Dinah. She is the uninvited guest. It is at this dinner that we learn about how the three individuals' circumstances will collide. Simon is out to prove Jesus is a fraud. Jesus will show up as He always does, All-knowing and gracious. Dinah came to worship Jesus. She worships as if they are the only two in the room.

The Blind Elite

Let's set the scene. First, we have Simon who is a Pharisee. A Pharisee is an elite group. This means they were some of the richest, most educated, and influential people of their time. They are a like-minded set-apart people who are devoted to religious purity. They are concerned with observing the oral traditions and the Law of Moses. The Pharisees were rigid in their adherence to specific behavior based on their own interpretation of the ambiguities or unclear parts of the Torah (the first five books of the bible). There is nothing wrong with being in an elite group or being devoted to purity. The problem comes when traditions are placed before God's people. They used their knowledge to suppress people. They used God's word to look down on and cast out those who they felt weren't worthy of God. This was not done just to "the Gentiles" but also to the chosen people of God, the Jews. If you did not meet their standards, you were rejected. Who were the rejected? The poor, the lame, the sick, the children, those of certain occupations, and women. The Pharisees saw Jesus as an ordinary man who claimed to be God. Their finite unbelieving minds and seemingly high knowledge of Torah blinded them to who Jesus was. They hurled accusations at Him and tried to discredit Him at every opportunity. They called Him a glutton and a drunkard, a friend of tax collectors and sinners. We get the opportunity to look back at that time and day, and we wonder, what was wrong with Jesus eating with tax collectors and sinners? If we bring it to our time, it is like seeing your Pastor having dinner with drug dealers and prostitutes. You would, or better yet, let's talk about me. If I saw my Pastor chopping it up at a dinner table with the D' boys and known streetwalkers, I would do a doubletake. However, knowing my Pastor's character, I know that if that was the case, he was trying to win them for Christ. That's just it, the Pharisees did not know Jesus' character, nor were they trying to get to know Him genuinely. In their minds, He was disrupting all that had been put in place and it was causing them to look bad. It was causing people to have a doubletake moment when looking at the Pharisees' character compared to this welcoming and accepting man, we call Jesus.

Knowing the character of the Pharisees, it is only logical to think that the only reason Simon would invite Jesus to dinner was to try to catch him up with a question-and-answer debate so that people would drop this awe-inspiring view of Jesus. However, little did Simon know that he would be the one caught up in his own demise.

Invitation Accepted

We have Jesus, the guest of honor or, should I say, dishonor. He is the one all eyes are on. Everyone always wanted to see what Jesus would do in any given situation. Not because they believed who He said He was but out of amazement at His behavior and rebellion against the traditions of the teachers of the Law. Why would Jesus show up to dinner with people who despised Him? What is the purpose of going to dinner with people who were always mocking or trying to degrade Him? The Pharisees are children of God too. They need salvation just like everyone else. For Jesus, this is his mission, to save the lost. And even though they didn't know it, they needed Jesus even more than the sick and lame. Jesus knew His time on Earth was limited and He did not have time to be petty, hold grudges, or seclude any particular people group. Guess what, neither do we. We don't have time to ignore, run away from, or hold onto past hurts. Tomorrow does not belong to us until we get there. We have no idea if we will wake up each day, nor if we will make it through the day. People who have lost their lives in car accidents had no idea when they woke up that morning, it would be their last. It is arrogant to believe that we are in control of what happens. We do not control any outcomes outside the very decisions we make or the reactions we have to our circumstances. Jesus wanted to reach all people groups. He desires that none perish but that all come to repentance, 2 Peter 3:9. Jesus loves us all and He came to earth to save all of us.

"For God so loved the world that He gave His only Son, that whoever believes in Him should not perish but have eternal life." (John 3:16)

Simon's heart could be changed if he was willing. If Simon could see past his self-righteous (morally superior) attitude and accept Jesus, everyone at the table was a potential victory. So, Jesus accepts, knowing full well how Simon's dinner party felt about Him. Jesus walked the earth in confidence because He knew who He was, and He knew Who He belonged to. We have this same right. We have the right to walk in confidence because we are the children of God. We are Kings and Queens. We are image bearers. Our confidence is not in ourselves but in the One who created us, the One who sent His Son to come and get us when we got lost. We don't have to be afraid of our circumstances or the people's faces. We need only do the will of our Father and delight in Him. That is the demeanor and attitude Jesus had as he sat to break bread with these lost men, these lost image bearers.

The Uninvited and Unwanted

Dinah wasn't supposed to be there. She was an uninvited, unwanted guest. First and foremost, women were not allowed to dine with men. In the first century, women were seen as second-class citizens, worth no more than animals. They were looked down upon, if looked upon at all. So, for Dinah to show up to this dinner was unheard of and completely inappropriate. Not to mention, she was known as a woman of the city, a sinner. This implies she was a prostitute. Dinah was going about her day as normal. She got up early, ate breakfast, and later in the day she headed into town. As she was walking through town, she kept her eyes averted as to not look anyone in the face. She could not take another nasty look from the people she walked past. They didn't know the things she suffered to cause her to lead her particular lifestyle. So, she kept her head down and pushed her way through town. On her way she overheard some men talking about Jesus. They said he had just arrived at Simon's house for dinner. She thought, "Jesus." The last time she had seen Him, he was so kind and loving towards her. She had to show Him how much she appreciated all that He had done. She wanted Him to know how the words He spoke impacted her.

Dinah runs home thinking, "What do I have at home that I can bless Jesus with?" On her way, her head was no longer looking down. She didn't care who looked at her with disdain or disrespect, she was on a mission. She had to get to Jesus. She enters her home, rushes to her bedroom, and looks around for something she can use to give to Jesus to show her gratitude. She grabs her best perfume. The one that she had been saving for a special occasion. As she picks it up, she smiles and says to herself, "This is a special occasion." Dinah rushes past the towns people heading to Simon's house where Jesus is. When she reaches Simon's house, there is no mention of her looking at, speaking to, or even considering anyone in the room except Jesus. She made a beeline to Him as if He was the only one in the room. She did not say a word. She spoke with her actions. She came prepared to serve and worship the Christ, the Savior, the gracious One. She was on a mission to show her affection, gratefulness, and honor to the One she knew to be the Son of God.

The Contrast

Looking at the stark differences between Dinah and Simon, we see they both wanted to be in the company of Jesus but for two entirely different reasons. One wanted to discredit Jesus and the other wanted to worship Him. Both of them were image-bearers Jesus had come to serve. For us, 21st-century believers, we scoff at Simon and sing praises about Dinah. But let's really look at this story closely. Who do you identify with, the sinner or the Pharisee?

As Christians, we have a bad habit of looking at others as if we are clean and they are dirty. As if we deserve Christ and they don't. We turn our noses up to those who do not fit within our perspective of worthiness. As if we have the authority to determine if someone is worthy when we ourselves are not. We approach people with long-handled spoons, keeping them at arms-length. We use or misquote scripture to discredit those who are rich in finances. such as *"... it is easier for a camel to go through the eye of a needle than for a rich person to enter the kingdom of God."* Matthew 19:24. We use the bible to beat people across the head when from the outside in it looks as if they don't have a relationship with Christ based on the way they live. The single mother who is frowned upon because she is seen as bringing her struggle upon herself. We have no idea what has caused her to end up as a single mother. Maybe if we got to know the woman and not her circumstances, we could have grace for her. The drug addict or alcoholic in our peripheral, we say if they really believed, God would deliver them. The woman who is unable to bear children or the person in a wheelchair is seen as the source of their pain. They must have done something for God to allow them to suffer. How we love to point our fingers at them, as the Pharisees did this woman. All the while Jesus is saying I love you, *AND* I love them.

We see suffering as a bad thing. Yes, it is painful. Yes, it is inconvenient. Yes, it shows our humanity. Yes, it causes us to be vulnerable when we would rather not. But guess what, it also causes us to mature and grow closer to God. It causes us to seek God, to lean in whether that is to receive comfort or strength. Jesus taught us what suffering looks like on the cross. He promised that there would be suffering but we could overcome it.

> *I have said these things to you, that in me you may have peace. In the world you will have tribulation (trouble, worry, anxiety, burdens, affliction, tragedy). But take heart, I have overcome the world. (John 16:33) (words added for emphasis mine)*

We must suffer to know Jesus. We must suffer to grow. We must suffer to reach our full potential. Without the suffering, there is no perseverance, resilience, or learned lessons. I have talked about the little puppy that changed my life. God loved me enough to allow me to suffer loss to restore my life. Without the suffering, I would still have eyes that were unseeing. I would still be numb, not able to fully enjoy my life and those in it. I would not be fully free to experience the goodness of God. My suffering has allowed me the ability to be a resource, a voice, and comfort for someone else suffering. How can we help others grow if we never experience the pain? How can we relate to those hurting if we never feel the sting of regret, betrayal, disappointment, tragedy, discouragement, or loss? It is through suffering that we can comfort others.

> *Blessed be the God and Father of our Lord Jesus Christ, the Father of mercies, and God of all comfort, who comforts us in all our affliction, so that we may be able to comfort those who are in any affliction, with the comfort with which we ourselves are comforted by God. For as we share abundantly in Christ's suffering, so through Christ we share abundantly in comfort too. If we are afflicted, it is for your comfort and salvation; and if we are comforted, it is for your comfort, which you experience when you patiently endure the same sufferings that we suffer. Our hope for you is unshaken, for we know that as you share in our sufferings, you will also share in our comfort. (2 Corinthians 1:3-7)*

Jesus walked this earth as a human so that He could understand our affliction. He felt what we feel. Hunger, fatigue, betrayal, love, loss, and finally death. He experienced it all so that He could empathize with us and as He sits at the right hand of the Father, He can intercede for us. He can say, Dad, this is what they were feeling. This is how they are suffering. This is what they are trying to overcome. Have mercy on them for my sake.

> *Since we have a great high priest who has passed through the heavens, Jesus, the Son of God, let us hold fast our confession. For we do not have a high priest who is unable to sympathize with our weaknesses, but one who in every respect has been tempted as we are, yet without sin. Let us then with confidence draw near to the throne of grace, that we may receive mercy and find grace to help in time of need. (Hebrews 4:16)*

Simon points his finger at Dinah, looking at her with disdain, "If this man were a prophet, he would have known who and what sort of woman this is who is touching him, for she is a sinner." Luke 7:39. Jesus is looking at her with love and compassion. Jesus knew exactly who Dinah was and from her response to Him, she already had an encounter with Him. What's even more important, unlike Simon, Dinah knew who she was and that she was unworthy. Simon was self-righteous and thought he was even better than Jesus. Dinah just wanted to show her gratitude. In fact, the sole purpose of her worship was gratitude. Simon's problem was that he didn't know who he was. Just like Dinah was suffering from whatever brought her to the point of her sin, he was suffering from sin as well. He was suffering from pride which made him blind to who was actually having dinner with him. The One who could save Simon was right there with him and it was as if he was a mute. His eyes were open but unseeing and ears open but unhearing all because he held himself in high esteem and should have been humbling himself instead.

An Opportunity to SEE

As I read through this particular scripture, I saw something I never saw before. I always saw this from the woman's point of view. The woman as the main character. Her plight and how she was looked down upon by the Pharisees. But now I see it differently. I challenge those of you reading this with a different perspective. What if this meeting was set up for Simon, not the woman? What if this was a divine appointment for Dinah to show up unannounced and uninvited so that Jesus could show Simon the way to freedom and salvation? Maybe this entire episode was Jesus showing compassion for Simon using Dinah as the avenue to reach him. Jesus did not have to show up to dinner. I'm sure there were several other invitations he received that He could have accepted, but He chose to accept Simon's. Let's look at the set-up.

Simon thinks to himself, "If this man were a prophet, he would have known who and what sort of woman this is who is touching him, for she is a sinner." Luke 7:40. Simon is saying to himself that Jesus is a fraud and not who He proclaims to be. Simon never uttered a word, but Jesus answered his thoughts. "Simon, I have something to say to you." Luke 7:40. Jesus began one of His famous parables. "A certain moneylender had two debtors. One owed five hundred denarii (20 months of wages), and the other fifty, (two months of wages). When they could not pay, he cancelled the debt of both. Now which one of them will love him more?" Luke 7:42 *(words added for emphasis are mine).* Jesus is known for asking questions. He does not ask them because He doesn't know the answer. He asks us questions because He wants us to ponder the question and get revelation. Simon responds with the obvious answer, "The one, I suppose for whom he cancelled the larger debt." Luke 7:43. What I love about this part of the parable is that the depth of the debt didn't matter. Both amounts were equally forgiven. Forgiveness is granted no matter the amount of the debt or sin. Jesus said, "You have judged rightly." Luke 7:43. Even though Simon answered the question correctly, he was still deaf and blind to the revelation. So, Jesus explains it to him.

Jesus looks at Dinah and speaks to Simon. He says, "I entered your house; you gave me no water for my feet, but she wet my feet with her tears and wiped them with her hair. You gave me no kiss, but from the time I came in she has not ceased to kiss my feet. You did not anoint my head with oil, but she has anointed my feet with ointment." Luke 7:44-46. What is Jesus telling Simon? He is saying to Simon, "You did not show me common courtesy when I entered your home." Why didn't Simon show Jesus the same courtesy he shows other guests who come to his home? The Bible does not present us with an answer. However, I believe Simon was concerned about his other guests and what they might think if they saw him offering Jesus the same courtesies they received. Or, going back to Luke 4:40, "... And he answered, "Say it, Teacher." Simon saw Jesus as no more than his equal or even beneath him. Either way, Simon disregarded his own tradition of cleanliness and hospitality because it was Jesus. Dinah on the other hand dropped all pretense to express her love, honor, and worship for Jesus. She did not care what people would say or how they would feel. Her only concern was her Savior, the one who had touched her heart and made her whole. So, Jesus uses Dinah as an example to Simon so that he has an opportunity to see with his spiritual eyes and change his heart. He says, "Therefore I tell you, her sins, which are many, are forgiven – for she loved much. But he who is forgiven little, loves little." Luke 7:47. What is Jesus trying to get Simon to understand? Forgiveness comes when our hearts can admit the sin within it. It is the heart posture that gains us the mercy of Christ. Sin is sin, many sins, or little sins, they all amount to sin and the penalty is death. It is only our human hearts that put measures on sin. Death is death. We don't have little death and big death. Dinah knew that she was a sinner and unworthy of Jesus' forgiveness and that is why her worship was so sincere. When we look at our lives compared to others, we think we are ok. But when we compare our lives to God, it gives a true picture of the wretchedness that lies within. God is the measuring stick, not people. When we say, "at least I don't do..." while looking at someone else, we have already started off wrong. "At least" is not good enough. Simon only needed to realize that the only reason Jesus took the time to come to dinner and tell the parable using Dinah as an example was because He loved Simon and wanted him to be free. He wanted Simon to experience the awe and wonder that Dinah had. Experience the freedom from the demands and weights of this world and the glory from the presence of God. Jesus is amazing. I am so glad that He will come and get us even when we don't know we need Him. Simon didn't know he needed Jesus, but Jesus did. Jesus knew that Simon would invite Him to dinner, and He knew that Dinah would show up and He knew that an opportunity would present itself so that He could reach this lost image bearer. Just like Simon, we are all given an opportunity to accept Christ as Lord and Savior or reject Him. My prayer is that if you have not accepted Jesus Christ as LORD and Savior, you will. Do not harden your heart but allow the Spirit of God to rest on you and change you.

"... Today, if you hear his voice, do not harden your hearts as in the rebellion, ..." (Hebrews 3:7-8)

Where God isn't moved by the quality of our voice but by the condition of our hearts.

Chris Tomlin

Reflection Questions

1. What do you think about the uninhibited way in which Dinah treated Jesus? Are you restrained or careful in the way you praise God?

2. In what way did Simon doubt Jesus? In what ways do you find yourself doubting who Jesus is or what He can do in your life?

3. How did Jesus express His love to Dinah and also to Simon? In what ways do you experience the love of Jesus?

4. What was Jesus trying to get Simon to understand with the parable of the canceled debt? How did Simon's view of Dinah show his unwillingness to forgive?

5. Jesus compared how Simon treated him compared to how Dinah treated him. Why do you think Simon didn't offer Jesus common courtesy as he did his other guests? What does this teach us about how we should honor and reverence Jesus?

____

____

____

____

CHAPTER 7

Not on the Sabbath

*But the ruler of the synagogue, indignant because Jesus had healed
on the Sabbath, said to the people, "There are six days in which work
ought to be done, come on those days to be healed, and not on the
Sabbath." Luke 13:14*

For three years Jesus ministered on earth. He healed the sick, made the mute talk, opened blind eyes, and redeemed those who were oppressed with deformities and demons. All the while, He was teaching "Repent for the Kingdom is at hand." Out of all these miracles and acts of love, He repeatedly and fervently tried to reach the hearts of the religious leaders. He loved them just as much as He loved all the others. Yet, they refused to humble themselves and receive sight, hearing, and redemption.

In chapter 13 of Luke's Gospel, Jesus teaches in a synagogue for the very last time before the crucifixion. And, just like the other times He is teaching, His message is geared toward the religious leaders whose hearts were calloused. He desperately wanted them to get it. They were the teachers of the word. Who more should get the spirit of the law than those who represent God? They were people of influence, and they controlled the narrative of how people lived and saw God. Jesus wanted people to see God not from a religious standpoint but from a relational one.

The religious leaders were so focused on religiosity that they missed relationship. I am not discounting religion as it is helpful to do things religiously. However, we must not forget why we do what we do and for whom we are doing it. Our hearts must reflect what we religiously do. I do not want to read my Bible because I have to or even need to. I want to read so that I can know, love, and honor God better. I want to know what pleases Him. And through knowing Him personally, I can begin to truly know who I am and why I exist. "Having the eyes of your hearts enlightened, that you may know what is the hope to which he has called you ..." Ephesians 1:18.

A lot of people know facts about God, but that is not enough to sustain us through the ups and downs of life. We need to know someone we can truly trust and believe has all power and can control the outcome of every situation. It is that kind of perspective that helps me get out of bed when all hell is breaking loose in my life, or I am hurting so bad from emotional or physical pain. I can lean my entire weight on the fact that if God allows something in my life that is causing discomfort, there is a reason for it, and it will be for my good.

The religious leaders taught about rules, for which they had added extra padding. This padding on the rules was meant to keep people from stumbling. I believe initially, the padding was done to help not to harm. Some Pastors do the same thing. They try to manage people's homes from the pulpit. They tell people what they can and cannot do based on their perspective instead of teaching God's word and allowing *it* to convict and change the hearts of people. It is the word that transforms people's hearts and ultimately their lives, not man. No matter how much people are preached at, if it is not grounded in the word, there will be no change, or it will be temporary at best. These leaders who add their own perspective and spin to God's word don't leave room for God's word to work. Instead, it causes the leader to get puffed up in pride and become self-righteous, looking down on those who cannot keep up with all the expectations placed on them. What they are stating may not be wrong, but it is not their place to govern what only God can govern. Let the word through the Holy Spirit do the work.

In this story, there is a woman, we will call her Rachel, who has suffered a debilitating condition for 18 long years. She shows up at church where you would expect to get healing. But she did not fit. She was not supposed to be there. She was not allowed.

Why? One reason is because she was a woman. The other reason is that she was imperfect. Sound familiar? We have some of the same dilemmas today. Women are supposed to be seen not heard. Anyone who comes into the church house and still has the stink of imperfection on them is shunned. Now, this is not every church, but this is what you will hear many people who don't attend church say. People who have tattoos all over them, those who have gender challenges, or practice homosexuality, or young people who are still trying to figure it out should be just as welcomed as those without these visible proclivities. The outward behavior or expressions are due to an underlying condition. There is something underneath that Jesus is trying to bring to the surface so that it can be healed.

We must not assume that everyone who does not look the part does not know or have a relationship with God. Most people see me and think, she knows the word and teaches the word, so she clearly knows and loves God. And this is true. However, I am bent toward certain appetites just like everyone else. I have demons that continue to seek me out and try to entrap me that I have to fight every day. I have to consciously choose between what I desire and the God I love. On most days I do very well, and on others not so much.

I had been fighting an on-again, off-again relationship with smoking weed until God revealed to me why I continue to go back to it. How it continues to entrap me. He showed me all the times I decided to go back and what my thoughts were. In my mind, I played with the idea that I didn't like being such a deep thinker, sometimes it is to a fault. I also have a serious nature which can be off-putting to some people. Because of these characteristics, a lot of people shy away from me. Yes, they love on me and show me kindness, but they don't want to get close. What I hear most is that "it feels like you are looking into my soul.", "It seems like you can see through me." Neither of which I can do. Because of this, I would say to myself, "I just want to be free and lighthearted. I don't want to be so deep. How can I take the edge off?" I would go from taking a little of the edge off to full-blown addictive behavior. I would be trapped all over again. Smoking and/or drinking to take the edge off of my guilt and then beating myself up for giving in. Round and round the merry-go-round I go.

One day, in my spirit, I heard God say, "You don't like you. You don't like what I created. I created you to be a deep thinker. I created your serious nature. Your voice was made to speak life into others which means you cannot do what others do. Embrace the you I made you to be." When I got that revelation, I sat in it and let it wash over me. It allowed me to move forward without looking back. I'm not saying that from here on out I will be a perfect human being, but what was underneath the behavior came to the surface. Once light had been shed on the darkness in my heart, the darkness had to flee. When you turn on a light in any dark place the darkness disappears. Turn on a light switch in a dark room and see what I mean.

If we continue to send people away or make them feel unloved and unwanted, then we have failed them and God. Jesus came to save the lost, the sick, and the hurting. When Jesus went to Matthew the tax collector's house for dinner, it ended up being a party of tax collectors and sinners. The Pharisees were upset because Jesus was eating with them. Jesus put them in their place though. He said, "Those who are well have no need of a physician, but those who are sick.... I desire mercy, and not sacrifice. For I came not to call the righteous, but sinners." Matthew 9:10-13. What is really sad about this event, is Jesus was offering salvation even to the Pharisees that were complaining. They thought they didn't need a physician. They did not know they were heartsick. Their minds were spiritually darkened and did not see that Jesus was offering them healing.

The Pharisees saw their security in knowing the Law. Reading and memorizing God's word is great, but it is not enough. John 5:39-40 says, "You search the scriptures because you believe in them you have eternal life; and it is they that bear witness about me, yet you refuse to come to me that you may have life." It is only through Jesus Christ that we are saved from the wrath of God. We must have revelation and wisdom. Our eyes must be enlightened so that we may know Him. Ephesians 1:18-19. Not to point the finger at them only, because I have been guilty of the same practices. Feeling like because I am reading the bible regularly and praying daily that I'm good. God is not interested in works without heart posture.

For God, it is the motivation behind what we do. So, we must consistently ask ourselves, "Am I reading, praying, working, going to church, etc. because I am seeking *Him* with my whole heart, or is this merely religiosity?" Do we want to know Him or what He can do for us? Ask yourself, "The thing I am doing right now, is it unto Him or is it for me to say I did it?" "I read the verse of the day to keep the devil away. I prayed today so that *my* day would go well." It should be, I met with my Father today by reading his word and having a conversation with Him.

Rachel was in the synagogue but must not have been there the entire time. She must have slipped in at some point because the men would have dismissed her before Jesus began His sermon. "Now he was teaching in one of the synagogues on the Sabbath. And behold, there was a woman who had a disabling spirit for eighteen years. She was bent over and could not fully straighten herself." Luke 13:10-11. Jesus was in the process of teaching and all of a sudden, this bent-over woman appeared. Some Bible versions say she was bent over double. Because she was out of place and unexpected, the sermon stopped. It would be like being in a church service, and while the preacher is preaching, a drunk and stumbling man began to walk up the middle aisle. The congregation's attention would veer from the preacher's message to the man in the aisle. In my imagination, this is how the listeners of Jesus' message would have responded. Some people would be very upset, seeing this as a disrespectful interruption. Some would feel disdain, as the obviously drunk man is interrupting their religious ceremony. I can literally see the people's faces. The upturned lips, disapproving stares, and disgusted *hmph* from their lips. They would wonder, who let this man in, instead of the obvious compassion he needed.

For a woman to show up where she was not wanted means she had to be desperate. She no longer cared what the men of the synagogue would say or how they would look at her. She was exhausted and wanted a different life. She wanted to be free. So, she went to the very place where healing should take place. She sought out the church where Jesus was. Isn't that what we do when we are tired of being sick and tired? We seek the One we hope can fix it. We seek Him with all the hope and faith we can muster and show up to the place where He is supposed to be. The church is supposed to be the place where people can find peace, love, acceptance, freedom, and redemption.

Rachel is bent over unable to straighten up. She can only see what's beneath her. There may have been several days where she would only see the ground and feet. Because she is a woman and deformed, she probably did not receive much compassion. She would have been shunned and disregarded, frowned upon, and looked down upon as less than. She could not see her own reflection on most days. She could not hold or hug her children or see their faces. Sometimes we walk around upright and are bent spiritually and emotionally. We carry so much weight from the world and life circumstances that it leaves us bent. The difference between us and Rachel is that she knew she was bent because hers was a physical bending. Ours is mostly unseen, we have no idea we are showing up every day bent. We are bent from the weight of money issues, work stresses, marriage problems, church hurts, worries about children, dysfunctional families, friendships and so much more. Rachel did what most of us will not, she took the weight of her struggle to Jesus. We in our independence try to work things out ourselves because the world says, "God blesses the child that's got his own." That is not God's message to us. He wants us to depend on Him and His guidance. He has the same message from the beginning when He told Adam not to eat from the tree of the knowledge of good and evil. He did not want mankind to rely on themselves to know what is good and what is evil. Instead, we are to place our trust in Him and He will guide us.

For those of us who are walking around bent, Jesus said, "Come to me all who labor and are heavy laden, and I will give you rest. Take my yoke upon you, and learn from me, for I am gentle and lowly in heart, and you will find rest for your souls. For my yoke is easy and my burden is light." Matthew 11:28-30. When I read this scripture, I see me carrying a very heavy bag. As I travel, I meet Jesus. He introduces Himself as the weight bearer. He takes the bag off my shoulders and places it on His own. He provides me with another bag that is just the right amount of weight for me. This bag does not cause a bend in my back or a hunch in my shoulders. There is a weight to carry when following Jesus, but the burden is light.

Unlike the synagogue ruler, Jesus showed compassion for Rachel. While others were sneering at her, or looking at her with contempt, Jesus called her to Himself. He said, "... Woman, you are freed from your disability." Luke 13:12. The word *woman* here seems terse but in the context of this event, Jesus is saying "Dear" or "dear woman". He uses the same word when speaking to His mother Mary when He changed water into wine. He said, "Woman, what does this have to do with me? My hour has not yet come." John 2:4. Jesus saw Rachel in her affliction, and He saw her faith. He did not ignore her or have someone send her away. He stopped His sermon to show her how much He loved her and how important she was to Him. He stopped during his journeys for other hurting people as well. Blind Bartimaeus stopped Jesus as He was traveling because of the sound of his cry. He cried out with a loud voice and would not be quieted. "Jesus, son of David, have mercy on me!" Luke 18:38. Jesus heard a sound of surrender and faith which made Him pause for the cause. Bartimaeus was about to be set free because he was willing to be go all in no matter what the naysayers had to say.

Most people in those times shied away from people who had disabilities or imperfections because they didn't want to be associated with someone who could be considered unclean or who may have committed some sin to cause their infirmity. But Jesus, being the loving God He was, "... laid his hands on her, and immediately she was made straight..." Matthew 13:13. We sometimes project onto God the response we expect from people. Since people will recoil at our deficiencies, we believe that God will do the same. So, we hide or run from Him. Sometimes we don't even consider Him as an option for healing or help. But God is not like us, He is very different than we are. In Him lies a degree of love that we won't fully understand until we meet Him in heaven. He is loving, compassionate, and unchanging. There is nothing more that we can do or undue for His love to change toward us. So, like Rachel, "we can come boldly to the throne of grace, that we may receive mercy and find grace to help in time of need." Hebrews 4:16.

Rachel showed up with all the strength she could muster knowing full well how she would be seen and treated. Because she did not let distractions deter her from the King, she was rewarded with freedom. The only way to receive true freedom is through a life submitted to Jesus. "... if the Son sets you free, you are free indeed." We must come to Jesus with our truth. Meaning, our naked, authentic, wretched undone, and broken selves, and He will set us free. We must come believing that "He exists and that He rewards those who seek Him." Hebrews 11:6. When we withhold our true selves from God, we forfeit a full and rich relationship with our Creator. He is seeking a relationship with the ones He created. He wants us to be honest with Him about everything.

Rachel came not just with her body but with her heart. Her heart carried her to Jesus and He touched her. I am looking forward to the day when I can physically touch Jesus. Now, I am learning how to touch Him spiritually. When I let my guard down and lay it all at His feet and then just abide or rest in His love, that is when He almost becomes palpable. I am surrounded by His presence. When my heart is poured out and emptied before Him, I can only describe feeling like I am sitting on my great-grandmother's lap, in her embrace in front of a warm fireplace eating a warm brownie and ice cream. I feel secure, comforted, loved, and accepted, and most times I don't want to leave. I wonder if this is how Rachel felt when He touched her. He called her, He looked at her, and He touched her. So often she had been overlooked or pushed aside as if she did not exist. Now, the King of kings sees her, and not only that He acknowledges her. She responds with a proper response. "... she glorified God." Luke 13:13. After 18 long years, Jesus healed her of her disability. She is set free through love, compassion, and a touch from Jesus.

I remember when I had Pustular Psoriasis. It is a form of psoriasis that forms on the palms of the hands and soles of the feet. I had huge pus pockets on the palms of my hands that would burst open, causing severe pain. It would then dry up and die. The skin would begin to peel. It would be like the Elmer's glue we would put on our hands as kids and then peel off for fun, except this was not fun at all. Psoriasis is a hereditary autoimmune disorder brought on by extreme stress or changes in the body.

Autoimmune disease happens when the body's natural defense system cannot tell the difference between its own cells and foreign cells, causing the body to attack normal cells.

I went to my personal care provider who thought it might be eczema, which I knew it wasn't. It kept getting worse and I was at a loss and didn't know what to do. I was finally sent to a dermatologist who gave me the diagnosis. I was relieved that there was a name for it. But, when she told me there was no cure, all my hope diminished and all I could do was cry. I was thinking, "I have to live this way for the rest of my life." I was devastated. They told me all I could do was manage my symptoms. I went through a battery of treatments trying to find the right one. I went from creams to ointments, to wearing protective gloves, to UV light treatments. The UV light treatment was very disruptive to my life. It was done three times a week, Monday, Wednesday, and Friday. I would come into the office and sit with my hands under a UV light machine to treat the pustules. My hands would improve all through the week but by the time Monday rolled around, it would be back to where it started. My hands had started to turn black from all the UV light. They were very rough, like a working man's hands. I was embarrassed for people to see my hands. I didn't even want to touch my husband. My husband was very loving and compassionate. He kept telling me he loved me and was not deterred by how my hands felt or looked.

One night at church the Pastor asked if there was anyone in the room seeking healing and I went to the altar. I had been praying and asking God to help me. So, when the opportunity presented itself, I went. I was so tired, and the doctors could not help me, so I decided to trust that this was my chance for true healing. When I got to the altar and the Pastor approached me, he asked, "Do you believe that God can heal you?" I told him I did. He told me, "It will not work without faith." I closed my eyes and told God that I believed He could heal me. I told Him that I would stop every treatment plan prescribed by the dermatologist as an act of faith. My healing was not immediate, but my hands did gradually begin to heal. A couple of months went by, and my hands were almost completely restored, minus a few spots.

My dermatologist was concerned because I had stopped all treatment and had not been in for a while. She asked me to come in for a follow-up appointment so that she could see the progress. She was amazed and asked what treatment I was using. I looked at her and said, "Prayer." She just smiled and said, "Whatever works." As I walked out of the dermatology office, I said to myself, "I will never come back to this place, and I receive my healing in the name of Jesus." This took place in 2015 and to this day I have not been back, and my hands are smooth and free from the disease. I take very good care of my hands with skin care products developed by my sister. But on that day in front of that altar, I received my healing just like Rachel received hers.

While Rachel is glorifying God for her healing, the synagogue leader is putting up a fuss. "But the ruler of the synagogue, indignant because Jesus had healed on the Sabbath, said to the people, "There are six days in which work ought to be done, come on one of those days to be healed and not on the Sabbath." Matthew 13:14. He is griping about Rachel's healing and Rachel is stretching her body in praise. I can see her bending over and straightening up over and over again with the biggest smile on her face and tears rolling down her cheeks. Being set free from what has had you bound is the most amazing experience. It is an encounter that you never forget and one that you will talk about for years to come. As Rachel walks home, she can see clearly all the things that have been distorted due to her inability to stand upright. That is a word for someone. When Jesus sets you free, your perspective changes. What used to be dark, cloudy, fuzzy, warped, and far away becomes crystal clear. It is like being unaware you are having vision problems because you have become accustomed to the lack of vision. Then you put on a pair of glasses, and everything becomes sharp, clear, bright, and beautiful. That is what my life feels like when I am far away from God, my perspective is dark, hazy, and twisted. I can see but I can't see. When I am open, honest, and dependent, my focus is clear, my ears hear distinctly, and my spirit is ready to receive what God has for me and for me to do.

This woman was literally bent over representing a life that is bent. Her story is a lesson for us. Life will, if we let it, keep us in a bent state. From this state, we see from a hindered perspective. We show up with a bent mentality. We engage with people from a bent reality. We need to come to Jesus daily, hourly, minute-by-minute to surrender the things that have us bent so we can receive healing. He is waiting with open arms for us to come to Him so that He can provide relief, love, comfort, and healing. When we come, I promise, you will rejoice just like Rachel. He sees you. He knows you. He loves you. He wants to set you free from whatever has you bound.

> *"So we do not lose heart. Though our outer self is wasting away, our inner self is being renewed day by day. For this light momentary affliction is preparing for us an eternal weight of glory beyond all comparison, as we look not to the things that are seen but to the things that are unseen. For the things that are seen are temporary, but the things that are unseen are eternal." (2 Corinthians 4:16-18)*

Whatever has been holding you back from lifting your head, Jesus has come to set you free.

Sharon Jaynes

Reflection Questions

1. In this story the Synagogue leader is concerned about not going against the tradition and order of service. In what areas have you found that you are more concerned about doing things religiously? Do the religious acts outweigh your compassion for people? If so, how can you do things differently?

2. What area(s) of your life are affected by living from a bent perspective? What do you need to do to surrender those areas to God?

3. Jesus said, "Woman, you are freed from your disability." Then He laid His hands on her, and she was healed. How does knowing that God sees you and wants to heal change your perspective about freely and openly coming to Him?

4. How can you show up for someone else who is bound, showing them the love and acceptance you received from God?

5. If you have some things that you need to surrender to God, speak to Him, write them out in a journal, or talk to a trusted friend. Doing one or all of these options will allow you to let it out and surrender it in confession. He wants to heal every area that has you bound.

____

____

____

____

Final Thoughts

The Breaking

*"We are God's handiwork, created in Christ Jesus to do good works,
which God prepared in advance for us to do." Ephesians 2:10*

In each of the stories we have discussed, all of the women went through a different breaking process. Through storytelling we got a glimpse of the painful circumstances of their lives. We saw how each woman went from pain to peace, or pain to deliverance, or pain to joy. God allowed their pain to be a testimony to each of us that, yes, we will have pain. And, yes, it is going to be uncomfortable, confusing, heart wrenching, and can make you downright mad. However, it is in this process we learn that the thing we are striving for will not bring us true success, but a deeper and richer relationship with Him will. Everything that is tangible will fade away but a true relationship with God is everlasting.

Hannah was emotional and depressed. She thought God was punishing her because she could not bare children. We saw how God showed her that even though He was with her in her despair, it was her surrender He was after, not her emotions. It was when she submitted her desire to have children to God that He was able to use her story to get the glory. This was the breaking for her. She had to realize that no matter how much she pouted, cried, and blamed herself or God, her emotions were not the pathway to her dreams. God is not a magician, a genie, or Santa Claus. She learned that for her, He was the Lord of Armies. He is *the* Mighty Warrior who has never lost a battle. When she leaned into Him, letting Him take the weight of her pain, she got off her knees and walked away with joy and expectation in her heart. God blessed her not only with a Son but with a genuine relationship with Him.

The Canaanite woman, Rebecca was desperate for her daughter's deliverance. She thought that crying out to Jesus would get her daughter delivered from what tormented her. Her request was not even specific, she only asked for mercy. She did not say, come to my house, or even lay hands on my daughter. She asked him to have mercy on her and told Him what she was dealing with. She acknowledged Jesus as God and with that she trusted Him to know what to do for her daughter. While Jesus heard her cries, surrender has a specific sound. It has a specific heart posture. For Rebecca it was begging on bended knee and Jesus comparing her to the family pet. Even that did not deter her requests. She simply told Jesus, "I'll take that if it will get my daughter healed, you can call me whatever you want." Her heart posture was humility, respect, honor, and belief that He could heal her baby girl. Rebecca's breaking is an example of letting go of our pride and feelings of entitlement. You may be asking but what is the sound? Is it a sound of trust, hope, or yielding of your own will for His? He hears you but He is listening for a tone of submission.

Liberty was concerned about her children. She was being threatened by creditors who wanted to take her boys to pay off an owed debt. Liberty sought out God for mercy through the prophet. She had lost the love of her life and was about to lose her boys who were her future. This situation was her breaking. God removed everything she depended on. Her only options were to give up or turn to Him for help. Most mothers will move heaven and earth for their children. So, even though she was furious with God for allowing these things to transpire in her life, she knew He could fix it. When God is the problem, only God is the solution. He will orchestrate or allow things in our lives that require us to see our humanness, our helplessness, our lack, causing us to relinquish our pride resulting in repentant, humble hearts. When Liberty surrendered control and went to the prophet, He took her lack and showed her His hand of grace and mercy. Along with provision, she received something she may have never acquired had her husband still been alive. A rich and authentic relationship with God. That is what He desires all of us. He longs for a genuine relationship with us. Isn't that amazing. The Creator of all things seen, and unseen pursues a relationship with us.

Deborah had already been broken but she still kept a spirit that was generous and kind. She had lost all hope and had given up on her deepest desire. God sent a man who would help her hope again. Although she had buried her dream in the depths of her heart, she did not let her pain cause her to lose her joy. She still enjoyed life and people. We have pieces of us that we have let die because those pieces cause us too much pain. Is it an absent father, a talent long forgotten, a health problem that has stolen the vibrance of life, or heartbreak that has turned to bitterness? There was a glimmer of hope shining through the crack of darkness and it was too compelling for Deborah to ignore. She decided to take a chance, come out of hiding and hope again. She was rewarded for her faith. God showed her that he had not forgotten about her and her kindness to the prophet had not gone unnoticed. If the thing you desired but buried has been resurrected in your heart, don't run from it out of fear. Pursue it and allow God to heal your heart in the process.

Paula had a situation that was dire. Her body was literally starving to death. God would show her through Isaiah that not only was her body dying, but so was her soul. All the other women we have discussed went looking for Divine help. Paula believed in Baal, the false god. That is who she worshipped and put her trust in for help during the three-year long drought. She had finally resigned to the fact that her god did not hear her. She did not go searching for the God of Elijah, He sought her out. He called Elijah to look for her in a foreign land for sustenance and shelter. He used a sad, dying widow who worshipped a fake god to feed His prophet. He, in turn showed Paula that He is the True and Living God. He saw her and loved her in spite of her misguided worship of a false deity. God comes for us even when we are not looking for Him. "But God shows His love for us in that while we were still sinners, Christ died for us." Romans 5:8. While we are chasing after worldly things to satisfy what only He can, He is pursuing us.

Dinah was compelled to worship. She heard Jesus was in her area and she broke all social customs to get to Him. She did not care about the onlookers or gossipers. When she arrived, she did not ask Jesus for anything or expect anything. She never said a word. Dinah was so grateful for the love that Jesus had shown her. She expressed her gratitude with fervor and was oblivious to anyone else in the room. Hers was a deep guttural need to be in the presence of her Savior. The One who saw her, loved her, accepted her. It is amazing to get lost in worship. When your spirit and God's spirit connect. There is no feeling like it in the world. It is a heavenly encounter with our creator. God has left an emptiness in us that only He can fill. Believe me, I have unsuccessfully tried so many things to fill that space. Food, weed, sex, friends, work, but nothing works or if it does it is fleeting. So, like Dinah, we can get into a space of wholehearted worship. It is when all of our barriers have been removed. Our barriers to zealous worship is a product of pride. Whether that is worrying about what someone may think, feeling unworthy, or believing it doesn't take all that. These are all indications of pride. Sometimes we have to tell our minds to shut up so that we can get into a place of surrender and gratitude. God is waiting on a heart posture that will welcome Him to join us in fellowship.

In the last story we have Rachel who is physically bent as an example to us of our spiritual bending. Rachel affords Jesus another opportunity to teach about relationship. The teachers and synagogue leaders focused so much on duties that they missed the main intent of the law. God established laws to teach the chosen nation how to interact with Him and to protect them from harm. Throughout the Old Testament, it is the Priests who are being taught to have love and compassion for the people. They were meant to serve the people, not the other way around. Everything had become about show and gain for profit. Despite this fact, God loved them as much as He loves all of His children. He wanted them set free from their pride and blindness. Rachel's interruption put Jesus in a prime position to rebuke the thought pattern of the synagogue leader.

Jesus encountered many who were lost and knew it, and quickly humbled themselves before Him. The elite were also lost but did not know it. They continued to exalt themselves which only created deeper graves. Jesus called them whitewashed tombs. "Woe to you, scribes and Pharisees, hypocrites! You are like whitewashed tombs, which appear beautiful on the outside, but inside are full of the bones of the dead and every kind of impurity." Matthew 23:27-28. They had the appearance of righteous men but were full of greed and discord. If only they would let go of their pride and open their eyes, they would see the goodness of God who sent His Son as a sacrifice for them. I used to be angry with the teachers of the law but as I have grown, it has turned to sadness. Today as I watch our world grow darker, I have learned to have compassion.

When there are scales over the eyes of man, Jesus is the only solution. And if He is rejected, freedom is impossible.

My season of breaking has been extremely disheartening at times, insightful at times, but it has led me into maturation. Above all, it has allowed me to put first things first and step out of idolatry. Relationships are more important to me than anything else. It is in relationships where I suffered the most. Losing my little Gracie, friends who I thought would be my ride or die forever, and my spiritual dad. I allowed all of these relationships to take my focus off the most important relationship.

In the grief from losing Gracie, I began to question God's love for me and the security I felt like He should have provided me. I thought if He did not protect me from any and all pain, that maybe He didn't love me like I thought He did. Maybe, I was not the apple of His eye. I felt rejected and abandoned by God when that was farthest from the truth. My friendships were my go-to for everything. In times of celebration or times of pain, the first people I would call would be friends. These humans may or may not have been happy for me. They may or may not have understood the difficulties I was experiencing. But God knows all and understands me better than I understand myself. He is the God who created comfort. How dare I look to created things before the Creator.

The break in my spiritual relationship has been the most arduous break. The relationship with my spiritual father was and still is very important to me. In the breaking of it, I could not put words to the emotions I was feeling until I went to visit a friend who began to tell me about her friend who had left a ministry that she loved. She used the words divorced, abandoned, and broken. Each word hit me harder and harder. I remember being a kid growing up in Richmond, California and some of my friends could jump up and do backflips and land on their feet. I thought they were amazing, and they could do it so effortlessly. One day I decided to try it. I was in my friend's front yard. It was a beautiful yard with a lot of green grass which I thought could be my cushion if I fell. She also lived right next door to me, so I could get help if I was hurt. She encouraged me with, "Come on, if I can do it, you can too." I finally agreed. I bent down, leaped up and flipped over. I was off to a good start. Then, something went terribly wrong. I unfortunately, did not jump high enough. There was not enough space between me and the ground so that I could get all the way around. So, when I came down, I landed flat on my stomach. I had heard about getting the wind knocked out of you, but I had never experienced it until that day. The pressure from my fall violently pushed all the air from my body as I hit the ground.

My friend's words knocked the wind out of me. I thought I had dealt with my pain but sitting there on her couch, I fought back tears as she told the story. When she looked at me, she saw my distress. I tried to fake it, but it was impossible, the pain was all over my face. I explained that I could barely hear the rest of the story because how those words affected me. I have daddy issues and I knew that going in. I don't know my dad. There is no picture I can refer to, no details I can conjure up. Nothing, nada. This pastor was very different than every pastor I had experience in the past. He did not want anything from me. He loved me, was concerned about me, and truly wanted me to grow. In ministry throughout my life, men have been an issue. They either wanted to use me for the gifts and talents I possessed or were sexually inappropriate. This was not the case with him. He had integrity and provided the fatherly love that I have desired for a lifetime. It was very intoxicating. Circumstances caused me to have to leave that body of believers. Here we go again, I had to grieve another loss. God began to show me why I needed to leave. He told me, I have always been and will always be your Father. You cannot replace Me with a human father. You must not look to the resource instead of the *Source*.

As I continued to go through that course of the breaking, I had to learn to do things differently. The coping mechanisms I used growing up were not healthy. "When I was a child, I spoke like a child, I thought like a child, I reasoned like a child. When I grew up, I put away childish things." 1 Corinthians 13:11. Instead of running, I began to sit in my emotions. When I wasn't sure what I was feeling, God found a way to show me. I allowed the emotions to sweep through me taking with it perfectionism, feeling the need to perform all the time, and imposter syndrome, not believing and walking in who God created me to be. As you move through the breaking periods of life, don't try to rush through it. Allow it to wash over you. Look at it as an opportunity to get to know yourself and God better. Relationships are built during times of adversity. Maturity and resilience are perfected in times of suffering.

Consider it a sheer gift, friends, when tests and challenges come at you from all sides. You know that under pressure, your faith-life is forced into the open and shows its true colors. So don't try to get out of anything prematurely. Let it do its work so that you become mature and well-developed, not deficient in any way. (James 1:2-4)

Topical Prayers

"Pray at all times in the Spirit with every prayer and request and stay
alert with all perseverance and intercession for all the saints."
Ephesians 6:18

Prayer for Identity

*"I will dwell in the secret place of the Most High, and I abide under the shadow of the
Almighty."* Psalm 91:10.

"I have favor with God and man." Luke 2:52.

"I am firmly rooted, built up, established in my faith, and overflowing with gratitude."
Colossians 2:7.

"I am chosen; specifically selected by God." Ephesians 1:4.

"I can quench all the fiery darts of the wicked one with my shield of faith." Ephesians
6:16

"I am an overcomer by the blood of the lamb and the word of my testimony." Rev 12:11.

"I am His elect, full of mercy, kindness, humility, and patience." Colossians 3:12.

"I am born of God, and the evil one does not touch me." 1 John 5:18.

"I will decree a thing and it will be established in my life." Job 22:28.

<u>Prayers for Adversity</u>

"I speak to every mountain in my life and command it to be removed and cast into the sea." Mark 11:23.

"Defend me from those who rise up against me." Psalm 59:1.

"I will call upon You when I am in trouble. You will rescue me and honor me." Psalm 50:15.

"All my needs are supplied according to the riches in Christ Jesus in glory." Philippians 4:19.

"Your grace overflows in my life. I have everything I need and enough to share with others." 2 Corinthians 9:8.

"Your goodness and mercy are following me, and I desire to dwell in the place of the Lord as long as I live." Psalm 23:6.

"I cast my cares on You because You care for me." 1 Peter 5:7.

"I receive trials with joy as they produce perseverance and maturity in me." James 1:2-4.

"I am not surprised when I suffer trials that test my faith, but I rejoice because I share in Christ's suffering." 1 Pet 4:12.

Prayers for Strength

"Let Your hand establish me and let Your arm strengthen me." Psalm 89:21.

"Let the power in Your hands be released in my life." Habakkuk 3:4.

"I am strong in the Lord and in the power of His might." Ephesians 6:10

"Let Your power work in me." Ephesians 3:20

"I do not have a spirit of fear, but of power, love, and a disciplined mind." 2 Timothy 1:7.

"Your grace is sufficient for me. When I am weak, you are strong. I will boast in my weaknesses so that the power of Christ may dwell in me." 2 Corinthians 12:9.

"I will submit to God and resist the devil." James 4:7.

Prayers for Protection

"I will dwell in safety; nothing will make me afraid." Ezekiel 34:28

"In the shadow of Your wings I will trust." Psalm 57:1.

"Lord, You are my shield and hiding place." Psalm 119:114

"No weapon formed against me will prosper and every tongue that rises against me in judgment, I will condemn." Isaiah 54:7.

"I take the sword of the spirit which is the word of God and use it against the enemy." Ephesians 6:17.

"I do not fear because You are always with me. You hold me up with Your righteous right hand. I am not afraid for You are my strength." Isaiah 41:10.

"You are my light and protection. You grant me favor and do not hold any good thing from me." Isaiah 84:11.

Prayers for Worship

"Lord, You made the earth by Your power, established the world by Your wisdom. By Your understanding stretched out the Heavens." Jeremiah 10:2.

"You are the true living God and the God of truth, the Everlasting King. The earth trembles at your wrath. Kings and nations are not able to bare your fury." Jeremiah 10:10.

"O' Lord, how excellent is Your name. You have set your glory above the heavens." Psalm 8:1.

"Who would not fear You O' King of the nations. It is fitting to You and Your due. All the wise of the nations cannot compare to you." Jeremiah 10:7

"Unto You O my strength, I will sing praises. For You are my Defense, my Fortress, and Hightower. You are the God that shows me love and unswerving mercy.

"Bless the Lord, O my soul, and all that is within me. Bless Your Holy name." Psalm 103:1.

www.ingramcontent.com/pod-product-compliance
Lightning Source LLC
Chambersburg PA
CBHW031447150726

47990CB00007B/2644